T0324375

LINCOLN'S
Man in Liverpool

LINCOLN'S
Man in Liverpool

Consul Dudley
AND THE LEGAL BATTLE TO
Stop Confederate
Warships

Coy F. Cross II

Northern Illinois University Press *DeKalb*

© 2007 by Northern Illinois University Press

Published by the Northern Illinois University Press, DeKalb, Illinois   60115

All Rights Reserved

Library of Congress Cataloging-in-Publication Data

Cross, Coy F.

Lincoln's man in Liverpool : Consul Dudley and the legal battle to stop
Confederate warships / Coy F. Cross II.

p.   cm.

Includes bibliographical references and index.

ISBN-13: 978-0-87580-373-9 (clothbound : alk. paper)

ISBN-10: 0-87580-373-3 (clothbound : alk. paper)

1. Dudley, Thomas H. (Thomas Haines), 1819–1893. 2. Consuls—United
States—Biography. 3. Lawyers—United States—Biography. 4. United States—
History—Civil War, 1861–1865—Naval operations. 5. Warships—Confederate
States of America—History. 6. Confederate States of America. Navy—
History. 7. United States—History—Civil War, 1861–1865—Claims.

8. United States—Foreign relations—Great Britain.

9. Great Britain—Foreign relations—United States.

10. Spies—United States—Biography. I. Title.

E467.1.D86C76 2007

973.7'22092—dc22

[B]

2006030944

Dedicated to my wife, Carol,

and to our children and grandchildren

CONTENTS

ACKNOWLEDGMENTS

When I began this endeavor several years ago, there had never been a published book dedicated to Thomas Dudley's efforts in Liverpool. In 2003, Stackpole Books issued David H. Milton's *Lincoln's Spymaster: Thomas Haines Dudley and the Liverpool Network*. After reading Milton's work, I realized he had focused only on Dudley as the leader of a spy network dedicated to stopping Confederate ships from sailing. While Milton writes an exciting account of Dudley as spymaster, I believe Dudley contributed much more to the Union cause. To me, Dudley was more than a spy, he was a lawyer determined to build a legal case strong enough to stop the Confederate ships. If he failed in this effort, he wanted to prove that British government failure to enforce its own laws allowed these ships to escape. So even after the ships sailed, Dudley continued gathering evidence against them. As a matter of course, he spent his entire tenure from 1861 until 1872 constructing the case the United States eventually used to gain a favorable settlement of its *"Alabama* Claims" against Great Britain. *Lincoln's Man in*

Liverpool: Consul Dudley and the Legal Battle to Stop Confederate Warships tells this larger story.

Many people have helped in making this publication a reality. The Huntington Library houses the largest collection of Dudley material, and the staff there created an environment that is every researcher's dream come true. The Pennsylvania Historical Society in Philadelphia houses records from Dudley's legal cases. That staff showed remarkable efficiency and patience in making their entire holdings available for review by a time-pressed and harried historian. One of the most appreciated gifts of time and energy came from the Camden, New Jersey Historical Society. I had set aside one day to visit Camden, but my schedule only allowed me to be there on a day the society's museum and collections were closed. The museum's executive director, Judith Snyder, and her intern Frank Caruso graciously used their day off to open their archives, make copies, and share their knowledge of Dudley and his family. The Beale Air Force Base Library staff repeatedly ordered microfilm of official records for me. Professor Emeritus Alexander DeConde, my mentor and friend, offered his expertise and sage advice. And, as always, I would like to thank my wife, Carol, and our five children and four grandchildren for inspiring and supporting me. They are a constant source of strength. To you all, thank you very much. I owe each of you a great debt of gratitude.

LINCOLN'S
Man in Liverpool

PROLOGUE

Abraham Lincoln's election as president in November 1860 prompted Southern states to carry through with their oft-threatened secession from the Union. By his inauguration on March 4, 1861, those states had established a government and selected Jefferson Davis and Alexander Stephens as president and vice president. Events moved swiftly. On April 12, Confederate General P. G. T. Beauregard ordered his troops to fire on the Union's Fort Sumter in the harbor of Charleston, South Carolina, and the American Civil War began. Four days later, President Lincoln ordered his navy to blockade Southern ports, thus making what he tried to define as a domestic disturbance into an international event. Perhaps if Lincoln had been better versed in international law, he might have chosen another course of action, but the new president had no experience with international affairs or diplomacy. What he did have, however, was a strong sense of purpose, a deep understanding of human nature, and a desire to settle differences peacefully, if possible.

In an international disturbance the secretary of state would play a principal role. Lincoln, wanting to strengthen his administration within the Republican Party, selected the party's leading politician, William Seward, for that position. The new president told his secretary of state, "I shall have to depend upon you for taking care of these matters of foreign affairs, of which I know so little, and with which I reckon you are familiar." Seward coincidentally had been Lincoln's primary rival for the presidential nomination. The well-traveled and well-read Seward understood foreign affairs much better than the president did, so in this sense he was an excellent choice. Unfortunately the new secretary saw himself as the administration's "prime minister" and often made rash statements—even suggesting they might provoke an international war to reconcile differences with the South. Seward publicly announced, "If the Lord would only give the United States an excuse for a war with England, France, or Spain, that would be the best means of re-establishing internal peace."[1] Lincoln, meanwhile, espoused "one war at a time," explaining, "after ending our war successfully we would be so powerful that we could call her [Great Britain] to account for all the embarrassments she had inflicted upon us." By midsummer 1861, however, Lincoln and Seward had evolved into an effective team as Seward gradually grew to appreciate Lincoln's "unique qualities" and to accept the president's overall responsibility and authority.[2]

Lincoln's announced blockade created a source of potential conflict with all maritime trading nations, but especially with Great Britain, the world's greatest sea power at that time and a nation largely dependent upon Southern cotton to supply its textile mills employing thousands of workers. To interact with the British government as the U.S. minister, Seward chose Charles Francis Adams, the son and grandson of former American presidents but a man whose qualifications rested more on education and family background than on his limited political and nonexistent diplomatic experience. Adams's father and grandfather had also been ministers to England, and during his father's tenure Charles Francis accompanied him and attended English boarding schools for several years. The younger Adams's calm disposition and dignified manner equipped him especially well to deal with Lord John Russell, the British foreign secretary who had a strikingly similar personality and bearing.

The Southern government created another likely source of conflict for the Union and Great Britain. As primarily an agricultural region, the South had developed little industry or shipbuilding. The Confederacy, therefore, would depend on outside help to survive. Because English mills relied on Southern cotton, Confederate leaders were convinced the British government would be forced to recognize the Confederate States as an independent nation. Otherwise, the idle and hungry industrial workers would revolt when the cotton stopped flowing. This reliance on "King Cotton" diplomacy severely hampered early Southern efforts to develop an international economy and limited the flow of vital military supplies.

Additionally, without shipyards, the South would have to turn to England to purchase or build the ships needed to break the blockade and create a Confederate Navy. Confederate Navy Secretary Stephen Mallory realized he had neither the time nor the resources to create a naval force comparable to the Union Navy. He would, therefore, focus on specialized ships to weaken and eventually destroy the blockade. Mallory's envisioned navy would include a few fast, self-sufficient ships, commanded by Confederate naval officers, to attack Northern commercial vessels. The cry from Yankee owners over these "commerce raiders" destroying the large Northern maritime fleet would force the Union Navy to give chase and thereby weaken the blockade. The other ships in Mallory's navy would be the virtually unstoppable, armor-covered ships equipped with the latest technology. The French and British navies had been perfecting this "ultimate weapon" for the past few years. Fitted with a long iron spearlike piercer on the bow and nearly impervious to conventional ships' firepower, these "ironclads" could easily ram and sink the wooden ships blocking entrance into Southern harbors. To purchase or construct his navy, Mallory dispatched several agents to Europe, one of whom, James Bulloch, proved an inspired choice. Bulloch had served in the U.S. Navy and afterward spent several years as a merchant captain along the Atlantic and

Gulf of Mexico coasts. He was intelligent, very knowledgeable about shipping and shipbuilding, both trustworthy and trust-inspiring, and dedicated to Southern independence.[3]

The British government, meanwhile, upon learning of Lincoln's announced blockade of the Southern ports considered its best course of action. Led by Lord Palmerston, a prime minister with extensive experience as foreign secretary, and Lord John Russell, a capable foreign secretary who had previously served as prime minister, the English cabinet recommended that the queen declare Great Britain neutral in the conflict and, given the area and population of the people in revolt, grant both North and South belligerent status, meaning they would be treated equally. England would enforce its Foreign Enlistment Act, which prohibited either side from equipping or arming warships within its ports and banned British citizens from enlisting on either side. Neither side's warships could change or increase armament in British ports. As a belligerent, the South could issue letters of marque to captains of privately owned ships and send them out as privateers to raid Northern merchant ships without their crews being hanged as pirates if captured; however, neither side could bring captured prizes into English ports for adjudication. The cabinet also suggested that the queen recognize the Northern blockade as legitimate, even though the 1856 Declaration of Paris (which all the world's major sea powers except the United States signed) stated, "Blockades, in order to be binding, must be effective; that is to say, maintained by a force sufficient really to prevent access to the coast of an enemy."[4] Whether through ignorance of the size of the Union's blockading force (eleven immediately available and serviceable vessels to cover more than three thousand miles of Southern coastline) or as a shrewd precedent for future use, English recognition gave the blockade international legitimacy and greatly benefited the North. The queen agreed with her cabinet's proposal and, on May 13, 1861, announced British neutrality in the conflict with the conditions the cabinet had recommended. Incidentally, the announcement came the very day Charles Francis Adams arrived in England to assume his post as minister. The following month, James Bulloch reached Liverpool, England's shipping and shipbuilding center, and immediately began creating Mallory's navy.

With Confederate shipbuilding activity centered in Liverpool, the Union consul position there would be second in importance in England only to the minister and arguably only slightly less important than the minister to France in all the rest of Europe. But neither Lincoln nor Seward immediately recognized how strategic the Liverpool consulate would be. The State Department did recall the pro-Southern incumbent but seemed in little hurry to install a replacement. Several weeks after accepting the post, Seward's first choice reconsidered and declined the appointment. Lincoln, then, without consulting Seward named Thomas Haines Dudley, a New Jersey attorney and state political activist, as repayment for his help in Lincoln's gaining the presidential nomination over Seward. Also offered the ministership to Japan, Dudley chose Liverpool because he believed medical treatment for a chronic bowel problem would be more readily available in England.

Like Lincoln and Seward, Adams and Dudley were contrasting personalities. While Adams descended from founding fathers, Dudley's ancestors were Quaker farmers. Adams's education included English boarding schools and Harvard whereas Dudley largely credited his widowed mother for his education. Adams respected and probably admired the British, but Dudley did not particularly like them and believed that nine-tenths of all Englishmen supported the South in its attempt to dissolve the Union. In bearing, Adams's dignity and quiet demeanor differed markedly from Dudley's passion and zeal. Dudley brought great energy and total dedication to his responsibility to thwart Confederate shipbuilding in Liverpool. He also meticulously gathered evidence against rebel activities and English complicity in those endeavors. Adams, in the dignified manner befitting an effective minister, presented that evidence to the British government and later used it to secure a favorable settlement in the "*Alabama* Claims." Dudley sometimes complained that Adams moved too slowly and Adams often believed that Dudley reacted too quickly. But, again like Lincoln and Seward, each seemed ideally suited for his position and they soon meshed into a powerful team. But would they be strong enough to defeat James Bulloch and Mallory's navy?

THE MAKING
OF A CONSUL

1

A cold blustery day greeted the *Africa* as she docked in Liverpool on November 19, 1861. Among her passengers arriving from the United States was Thomas Dudley, a "tall well-formed gentleman," his wife, Emmaline, and their children, twelve-year-old Edward and his younger sisters, ten-year-old Mary and seven-year-old Ellen. Dudley, the newly appointed consul for Liverpool, would soon be battling in the American Civil War's most important diplomatic arena. To add to his difficulty, Confederate agent James Dunwoody Bulloch had been in active service in Liverpool since the previous June. There was little in Dudley's background to indicate he was prepared for his daunting responsibility.[1]

Thomas Haines Dudley was the product of several generations of New Jersey Quakers. Born in Evesham Township, Burlington County, on October 9, 1819, he was the youngest of Evan and Ann Haines Dudley's four children. Evan died just five months later in March 1820, leaving Ann alone to raise the children on the family farm. Thomas attended the district school but credited his mother's teachings for his later success. Much of his education and his love of learning came from Ann's home schooling. She instilled in her children Quaker values including honesty, clean conscience, service to others, and education. Hard work and a simple lifestyle undoubtedly were an integral part of the Dudley home.[2]

Although Thomas early aspired to becoming an attorney, he could not afford to devote all his time to study. So he taught school for a few years, saved part of what he needed, and mort-gaged his farm for the rest. He then apprenticed with William N. Jeffers, a prominent Camden attorney, before passing the state bar in 1845. As Dudley prepared for the bar, he still found time for ro-mance. At twenty-four years old, he was handsome, with dark wavy hair and a full beard, and stood six feet tall. Emmaline Mat-lack, an attractive woman with brown hair and blue eyes, was a year younger than Thomas and eight inches shorter. They married in a simple Quaker ceremony on March 4, 1846. Their first son, Henry, named for Thomas's political idol Henry Clay and like Clay nicknamed Harry, was born the following year but died soon after his second birthday. Edward, Mary, and "Ellie" soon filled the Dudley home with other tiny feet and children's laughter.[3]

Thomas Dudley's law practice provided investment funds for a hotel and several lots in newly developing Atlantic City. He sold the hotel for $40,000 in 1859, a large sum at that time. In-come from his practice and investments allowed him to travel to Europe for his health, which seemed delicate throughout his life. In 1855 he visited Brussels, Zurich, Paris, Rotterdam, and sailed on the Rhine. Apparently his family did not travel with him. An accident in March 1856 probably compounded his health problems. Dudley was aboard the ferryboat *New Jersey* traveling between Philadelphia and Camden when the boat caught fire. He recalled hearing the screams from "the compact mass of human beings [in] back of me and they were on fire, lit-terly [sic] being roasted and burnt up alive. Such screams of agony and despair I never heard before and pray God I may never hear again."[4] Dudley jumped into the icy water and was rescued after about fifteen minutes. Fifty others perished. He later told a friend that he had "suffered much more mentally than bodily." Unspecified health problems prompted another trip to Europe in 1861 before his appointment as Liverpool consul. Throughout his tenure he needed periodic breaks to restore himself. Interestingly, his health influenced his decision to accept the appointment to Liverpool.[5]

Although the Dudleys were well respected and prosperous community members by 1861, it was not Thomas Dudley's education, law practice, or diplomatic ability that earned his appointment to Liverpool as consul. A lifelong Whig, he had served in various state and local offices since his youth. When the Whig Party died after the 1854 election, he moved to the new Republican Party for national politics. Locally he joined with former Whigs, a faction of the Native American or "Know-Nothing" Party, and Republicans in the anti-Democratic "Opposition Party of New Jersey." By 1860 the Opposition Party had merged into the Republican Party and Dudley became chairman of the Republican State Executive Committee of New Jersey.[6]

Dudley and other Republicans approached the coming election with a sense of anticipation. As an amalgam of antislavery parties and factions, the Republican Party had done well in its first national election in 1856. Party leaders knew that success in 1860 lay in nominating a candidate who could carry at least two of the four key states of Illinois, Indiana, Pennsylvania, and New Jersey, states that had voted Democratic in 1856. Although New York Senator William Seward was the leading Republican candidate and the most likely presidential nominee, many party leaders doubted he could carry any of the four key states, each of which preferred its own favorite son. Illinois and Indiana supported Abraham Lincoln, Pennsylvania was for Simon Cameron, and New Jersey wanted William Dayton, who had been the Republican vice presidential nominee in 1856.[7]

Thomas Dudley attended the 1860 Republican convention in Chicago as a New Jersey delegate-at-large, backing Dayton for president. With little support for Dayton outside New Jersey, state delegates were not committed to vote for him, in fact some planned to endorse Seward. Seward had tremendous support, especially in New England, but he had endorsed issues and made statements that alienated other regions, especially the four pivotal states. Seward's New England supporters, therefore, were more concerned with winning the election than clinging to their candidate and were willing to support any candidate whom the four critical states agreed upon. But these key states could not reach a consensus. Eventually Dudley suggested the four states poll their delegates to determine which candidate had the most support among them and then back whoever proved the strongest. This broke the deadlock. The four states settled on Abraham Lincoln, the New England states followed suit, and Lincoln quickly captured the nomination.[8]

The exertions of the campaign and the aftermath aggravated Dudley's "chronic bowel complaint." After nearly three months of illness, he followed his doctor's advice and again sailed to Europe for his health, probably leaving in late May 1861 and arriving in London in June. While visiting the American legation, he undoubtedly heard the news that the Confederacy had sent James Dunwoody Bulloch to England. New York newspapers described, in detail, what was supposed to be Bulloch's secret mission to buy commerce raiders to prey on Northern merchant ships. This must have been a hot topic of discussion and speculation around the legation.[9]

After London, Dudley traveled to Paris to see his old friend Dayton, the newly appointed minister to France. Dayton imposed upon him to serve as interim consul there. The previous consul, a suspected Southern loyalist, had left the post vacant and Seward's appointee, John Bigelow, had not yet arrived. Dudley filled the position from July 5 until August 23, when illness forced him to leave Paris for home. In April 1861, before leaving for France, Dayton had tried to secure a permanent position for Dudley, but war preparations in Washington overrode all other considerations.[10]

David Davis, Lincoln's friend and political advisor who worked with Dudley at the Chicago Republican convention, had in the meantime complied with Dudley's request for a diplomatic post and written Lincoln soliciting a position for Dudley. Dudley's friend William Newell recalled later that he, too, had interceded with Lincoln on Dudley's behalf. In a personal interview, after Dudley's return from Europe, the president informed him there were only two positions left worthy of him, minister to Japan and consul in Liverpool. Although the Liverpool post would be one of the Union's most critical diplomatic positions, it had been vacant since March 4 when Beverly Tucker, a President James Buchanan appointee and Southern sympathizer, had resigned. Anticipating that the rebellion would soon be over, Lincoln and Seward did not move quickly to fill the Liverpool post, and Seward's first choice declined his commission six weeks after accepting it.[11] Henry Wilding, the British vice consul, had been filling in. Lincoln offered Dudley the Japanese minister position, saying he had already promised Liverpool to his friend Illinois Governor Gustave Kroener. Dudley explained that, because of his health, he much preferred Liverpool where good medical help was available. Lincoln acceded and named Dudley consul to Liverpool without consulting Secretary of State Seward. Seward, although well aware of Dudley's role in Lincoln's nomination, became Dudley's solid ally after the latter became consul. Assistant Secretary of State Frederick W. Seward, the secretary's son, signed Dudley's appointment letter on October 15, 1861, and Secretary Seward issued the formal commission on October 25. The new consul left Camden just eleven days later, on November 5, and sailed for Liverpool on the 6th.[12]

England's November wind was not the only chilly reception to greet Dudley in 1861. Liverpool was a prosperous commercial and shipping center of 438,000 people that profited from close relationships with the American South. The slave trade financed the city's growth from a struggling port to one of the richest trade centers in the world. Trade in cotton and textiles replaced slaves after Great Britain ended slavery within her empire in 1833. By 1858, 96 percent of the cotton entering the United Kingdom passed through Liverpool and 83 percent of that cotton came from the American South. Liverpool brokers bought and sold Southern cotton, Liverpool merchants furnished Southern homes and clothed Southern planters, and Liverpool banks granted the credit that kept the Southern economy flourishing. Dudley later recalled that a feeling prevailed in the city that the North could never "suppress" the rebellion and the only alternative was to "permit the South to sever the Union."[13]

Several Liverpool businesses had established branch offices in Charleston, New Orleans, and other Southern cities. Conversely, a considerable number of Southerners found business opportunities in Liverpool, forming a sizable colony there by November 1861. The banking firm of Fraser, Trenholm and Company, for example, was affiliated with Trenholm Brothers of New York and Charleston's Fraser and Company. Throughout the war, Fraser, Trenholm and Company acted as the Confederate financial agents in Europe. The company accepted Confederate drafts, guaranteed contract payments, acted as clearinghouse for Southern loans and bonds, and provided financial advice and office space for Confederate agents. The company contracted for a ship that it planned to donate to the South to prey on Northern commercial shipping. A senior partner in the Charleston office, George Alfred Trenholm, even became secretary of the Confederate States Treasury in July 1864.[14]

Not only were Liverpool's business and commercial interests strongly pro-South, the community's press and political leaders had Southern leanings, too. Four of the city's five newspapers were overtly sympathetic to the Southern cause. Of the area's three members of Parliament, the first, John Laird, owned Laird and Sons, the shipbuilders who would construct warships for the Confederacy; the second, Thomas Horsfall, fiercely attacked any government attempt to interfere with Confederate purchase of ships or other war materials and possibly had connections to the Mersey Iron and Steel Company, which did a brisk business with the South; and the third, Joseph Ewart, though claiming to be neutral, also leaned toward the Confederacy.[15]

People throughout the rest of England initially supported the North in its perceived war against slavery, but many soon accepted Lincoln's repeated assertions that this was a war to preserve the Union and, therefore, shifted their allegiance to the South. The American minister in London, Charles Francis Adams, in his first dispatch to Secretary of State Seward remarked on "the cotton culture" that heavily influenced Liverpool's favoring the "disaffected." A few months later the minister's son and secretary, Henry Adams, commented, *"Their* merchants and friends in Liverpool have been warm and vigorous in their support from the beginning. *Ours* have been lukewarm, never uttering a hearty word on our side." Dudley probably already knew what to expect upon arrival, but he later recalled he landed in Liverpool with an open mind.[16]

A consulate clerk met the Dudleys and took them and their luggage to Mrs. Blodget's boardinghouse, where they had rooms reserved. A short time later, Henry Wilding called at the boardinghouse to greet the Dudleys and to transfer responsibility to the new consul. After a short discussion on pay and responsibilities, Dudley asked Wilding to continue as vice consul. The new consul formally took responsibility for the office the following morning, November 20, 1861.[17]

Dudley immediately notified Charles Francis Adams that he had arrived and assumed his duties in Liverpool. Although their backgrounds and temperaments differed, Dudley and Adams would form an effective team. The Dudleys were farmers of modest means, little known outside their community. The Adamses were among America's most distinguished families and included two presidents. Thomas Dudley's experience hardly qualified him to be consul. Charles Francis Adams was uniquely qualified to be minister, since his English boarding-school education, years living in England, and reserved temperament gave him much in common with Great Britain's ruling class. Dudley described himself as "self-reliant" and "quite likely . . . too zealous." Adams, in contrast, displayed a coolness that bordered on stiffness. Lord John Russell, the English foreign secretary, considered Adams "calm and judicious" and "very quiet and reasonable."[18]

Dudley later explained to a fellow consul the course he would follow at Liverpool. He would "studiously avoid" mixing in British politics but would take every opportunity "so far as [he] could so demean [him]self" to "set the public opinion right" about Northern institutions and the "present unhappy difficulties which exist there." For Dudley, in the Southern rebellion, unlike any other in history, the oppressors rose up against liberty. "It is to destroy the best, purest and freest government that the sun shines upon a government by the people for the people to build upon its ruins an immense slave empire."[19] His would be a formidable task. As John Bright, a Liberal member of Parliament, explained: "There are two nations in England, the governing class and the millions who toil, the former dislike your republic, and their organs incessantly misrepresent and slander it, the latter have no ill feeling towards you, but are not altogether unaffected by the statements made to your prejudice." Dudley came to accept Bright's assessment. As he wrote Secretary Seward, "the great mass of the residents of [Liverpool] is and has been against the North and in favor of the South. This feeling . . . is now deep and bitter."[20]

Immediately after Dudley's arrival, word came of events that nearly ended his stay almost as soon as it began. He had been consul just eight days when news reached Liverpool that a Union sea captain had stopped the British ship *Trent* in international waters and forcibly removed two Confederate passengers. The *Trent* Affair had begun to unfold earlier, when sixty-two-year-old Captain Charles Wilkes was returning the steam sloop *San Jacinto* from its West African station. When he discovered that James Mason and John Slidell, Confederate commissioners bound for Europe, had booked passage on the *Trent* for November 7, Wilkes decided to capture them.[21]

He halted the *Trent*, about three hundred miles east of Havana, by firing a shot across her bow shortly after noon on November 8. Wilkes gave orders to arrest Mason, Slidell, and their two secretaries, confiscate their baggage and dispatches, and make a prize of the *Trent*. Lieutenant D. MacNeill Fairfax searched the *Trent* but could not find the dispatches, which had been concealed in the British mail. The *Trent*'s captain also refused to produce a passenger list or other ship's documents. This refusal gave Fairfax the right to seize the ship and take her to a Northern port where an admiralty court could decide whether the Confederate emissaries and their dispatches were contraband and subject to confiscation. Fairfax, however, in a show of goodwill, used "a token display of force" to arrest and transfer the commissioners to the *San Jacinto* and released the *Trent*. In so doing, the lieutenant acted as his own court and violated international law. This violation would become the point of contention between the United States and Great Britain.

Captain Wilkes sailed north with his prisoners, landing at Fort Monroe, Virginia, on November 15, 1861. He immediately told reporters he had acted on his own initiative. He forwarded his report to Washington by a special train, where Secretary of the Navy Gideon Welles quickly carried it to President Lincoln. Wilkes and the *San Jacinto* carried his prisoners on to Fort Warren near Boston where a hero's welcome awaited the captain. The lack of military victories and the hatred for these particular prisoners invoked widespread jubilation in the North. Parades, banquets, and a congressional resolution praised Wilkes for his heroism.

Word of the incident reached Liverpool on November 27. Although a partial transatlantic cable connected Ireland and Newfoundland in 1858, it soon failed, and a successful cable did not span the Atlantic until 1866. Transatlantic communiqués traveling by ship required at least twelve to fourteen days. Upon hearing the news, Dudley wrote Secretary Seward, "The seizure of Mason & Slidell on board the Trent has created an excitement here which I never saw equalled. . . . The feeling is almost universally adverse, & very bitter."[22] Minister Adams recognized the gravity of the situation and expressed doubt that his tenure in London would last another month. On November 30, Prime Minister Lord Palmerston and Foreign Secretary John Russell voiced their government's outrage, calling Captain Wilkes's action "an act of violence . . . [and] an affront to the British flag and a violation of international law."[23] Russell then instructed Lord Lyons, the British minister to the United States, to demand the immediate release of Slidell and Mason and a suitable apology from the United States. Should the United States not comply, Lord Lyons was to withdraw and return to England. Great Britain, meanwhile, prepared for war. In a move to ensure that its own troops had adequate supplies while depriving the Union Army, the British government banned the export of saltpeter, small arms, ammunition, and lead, materials previously allowed because civilians also used them. Dudley wrote Seward of troops and military stores sailing for Canada and the call-up of some reserve forces and the alerting of others. Although England did not want war with the United States, she prepared for that possibility.[24]

The United States learned of the British reaction and war preparations on December 16, and Lord Lyons officially delivered Russell's message to Secretary Seward on December 23. During the cabinet meetings called to discuss the response to the British communiqué, the president suggested a plan for arbitration. It was Seward, however, who presented the solution that was finally accepted: he would release Mason and Slidell, acknowledging that Wilkes should have brought the *Trent* to port for adjudication, but also write a letter to Foreign Secretary Russell justifying the capture of neutral vessels carrying agents of an enemy. The release of the Confederate commissioners on January 1, 1862, defused the crisis, and relations with England gradually improved.[25]

The anti-Union feelings that the perceived affront aroused in England, especially in Liverpool, persisted throughout the war, however, and only added to Dudley's difficulties. The city would soon become the European center of Confederate wartime activity, especially shipbuilding. The new consul's first challenge was the *Oreto,* a Confederate warship already well underway in the William C. Miller and Sons' shipyard.

THE *FLORIDA*

―――― ◆ ――――

*"The first foreign-built
Confederate
cruiser"*

2

The reception that awaited James Dunwoody Bulloch, when he arrived in Liverpool on June 4, 1861, contrasted from Dudley's arrival five months later as dramatically as June's weather differed from November's. A warm sun greeted the Confederacy's chief purchasing agent and the man who would be Dudley's nemesis throughout his tenure as consul, as he stood on the deck of the steamer *North America* from Montreal, Canada. Bulloch was shorter and stockier than Dudley, and although two years younger, premature baldness and years at sea made him look older. Long sideburns that merged with a full mustache added to his dignified appearance.[1]

Bulloch had left Montgomery, Alabama, the Confederate capital, on May 9 and traveled overland to avoid the Northern blockade gradually encircling the South. He later recalled the South had "no machine shops, nor yards, no ship-wrights, and no collection of material for ship-building." Within the entire Confederacy, there was not a "single private yard having the plant necessary to build and equip a cruising ship of the most moderate offensive power." Stephen Mallory, the Confederate Secretary of the Navy, empowered Bulloch to purchase or have built several commerce raiders, ships that could create such havoc with the Northern merchant fleet that Union Navy Secretary Gideon Welles would be forced to divert warships from the blockade to give chase.[2]

Mallory had selected the right man for the job. James Dunwoody Bulloch, born near Savannah, Georgia, on June 10, 1823, moved to Roswell, near Atlanta, at an early age. He entered the U.S. Navy in 1839 and served until 1853, when he resigned and joined the merchant marine. After leaving the navy, he resided in New York and captained the privately owned mail steamer *Bienville* on the run between New York and New Orleans. On April 13, 1861, he was in New Orleans, preparing to sail the following morning. Rumors of the impending war circulated throughout the city. About 10 o'clock that morning, confirmation came that General P. G. T. Beauregard had fired on Fort Sumter in Charleston harbor.[3]

In April 1861, Bulloch had no property or any pecuniary interest in the South. He was a private individual who "completely identified with the shipping enterprise of New York." His "head" and "heart," however, were in the South. Upon hearing the news of Fort Sumter, he immediately wrote Confederate Attorney General Judah P. Benjamin offering his services to the Confederacy. Bulloch explained that he commanded the *Bienville* and needed to return her to her owners in New York, he then would be available for service. After mailing the letter, he returned to his ship and made ready to sail the next morning.[4]

Later that afternoon two members of the local "Board of War" visited Bulloch on the *Bienville* offering to buy the ship for the Confederate naval service. He declined, stating he had no authority to sell the ship. After further futile discussion, they informed him that if he did not accept their offer they would ask the Louisiana governor to confiscate the *Bienville,* by force if necessary. Bulloch felt torn: he could not give up his ship without resistance, and he did not want to use violence against the Confederacy to which he had just volunteered his services. He decided he would slip the *Bienville*'s mooring lines and make a run for it if anyone attempted to capture his ship. He learned later that day the governor had referred the matter to the Confederate capital at Montgomery, Alabama, and there would be no attempt to take the *Bienville* by force. The following day, April 14, word came from Confederate President Jefferson Davis not to detain the ship, "we do not wish to interfere in any way with private property."

Bulloch immediately sailed for New York, by way of Havana. Upon reaching New York on April 22, he learned the federal government had chartered the *Bienville* to carry troops to protect Washington, D.C. He immediately submitted his resignation. The following day he received Benjamin's letter summoning him to Montgomery without delay to see the navy secretary. Bulloch spent the next ten days winding up his affairs with the shipping company and attending to other business matters. Not wanting to reveal his intention and risk detention, he told friends he was considering a trip to Philadelphia and possibly on to Cincinnati, Ohio. Carrying just enough luggage for a few days, he traveled by train to Cincinnati, then by riverboat to Louisville, Kentucky. Feeling safe in Kentucky, Bulloch caught a train for Nashville, Tennessee, and then on to Montgomery, arriving near midnight on May 7. He noticed that, despite the late hour, no one seemed to be sleeping. Everyone was talking about and preparing for war.

Early the next morning Bulloch reported to Secretary Benjamin, who immediately introduced him to Navy Secretary Stephen R. Mallory, the former Florida senator. Bulloch recalled, "No useless phrases were employed in the presentation. [Benjamin] 'Mr. Secretary, here is Captain Bulloch.' [Mallory] 'I am glad to see you: I want you to go to Europe. When can you start?' [Bulloch] 'I have no impedimenta, and can start as soon as you explain what I am to do.'"

Mallory quickly described the Confederate Navy's lack of shipbuilding facilities and explained his plan. He considered it of "prime importance" to get commerce raiders to sea as quickly as possible to sink Northern merchant vessels. Mallory anticipated Union business interests would then compel Navy Secretary Welles to withdraw warships from the blockade to pursue the commerce raiders. Mallory and Bulloch discussed the type of vessel best suited for commerce raiding and the possibility of buying or building several of these ships in England. The secretary also authorized Bulloch to purchase and ship all possible naval supplies. He suggested that Bulloch consider the matter overnight, commit the important information to memory, and formulate any questions he might have.

The following morning, May 9, Mallory advised Bulloch to familiarize himself with the "nature and scope" of the British Foreign Enlistment Act and Proclamation of Neutrality to avoid embarrassing Confederate agents who were working to secure diplomatic recognition of the Confederacy. Mallory directed Bulloch to contact Fraser, Trenholm and Company, the Confederacy's bankers in England, and William L. Yancey and Dudley Mann, the Confederate commissioners in England. The secretary finally authorized his agent to exercise "wide discretionary power within the limit of his general instructions."

Bulloch left Montgomery by train that same night. Before crossing into Kentucky he memorized and then destroyed all his notes rather than risk their falling into Northern hands. He continued to Louisville and then on to Detroit, Michigan, where he crossed into Canada. From Windsor, the Grand Trunk Railway carried him to Montreal. He sailed from Montreal aboard the *North American,* arriving in Liverpool on June 4, 1861.

As the *North America* steamed up the Mersey River, Bulloch, with the bearing of a military man, stood on deck and surveyed Liverpool's world-class shipbuilding facilities. His demeanor reflected fourteen years in the U.S. Navy and another eight as captain of commercial ships. Experienced eyes surveyed the nearly five miles of "quays, docks, landing platforms, and dockyards" stretching along the riverfront. The Mersey teemed with maritime activity with tugs, barges, and ships from all over the world coming and going. Liverpool boasted several shipyards, including John Laird and Sons and William C. Miller and Sons. Bulloch must have been encouraged by what he saw.[5]

Early on the morning after his arrival, without official papers or credentials, Bulloch presented himself to Fraser, Trenholm and Company officials. Even though the Confederacy had not alerted its agents to expect Bulloch, they received him with "cordiality" and "trust." Charles K. Prioleau, the resident partner who would become Bulloch's loyal ally, authorized him to place his most pressing orders for ships and armaments and guaranteed payment, although the company had received no funds or authorization for the mission. Bulloch recalled, given Prioleau's endorsement, "Within a month after my arrival, I had not only been able to buy a fair quantity of naval supplies on their credit, but had laid the keel of the first foreign-built Confederate cruiser, and she was partly in frame before the Navy Department had found it possible to place any funds in Europe."[6] This first ship would be known as the *Oreto* during construction and then be commissioned as the C.S.S. *Florida*. Six weeks later, funds finally arrived and Bulloch contracted for a second vessel.

Although Liverpool's shipbuilders could easily accommodate Bulloch's requirements, he faced a major hurdle before he could obtain the commerce raiders. Great Britain's Foreign Enlistment Act of 1819 forbade the equipping and arming of ships in British ports for use of belligerents with whom that country was at peace. The Confederacy wanted to acquire a fleet of warships, naval weapons to arm them, and crews to man them. Determined to accomplish his purpose without violating British law, Bulloch consulted F. S. Hull, a leading Liverpool solicitor. "He piloted me safely through the mazes of the Foreign Enlistment Act, in spite of the perplexing ambiguity of its 7th Section, and the bewildering iterations and reiterations of the precept not to 'equip, furnish, fit out, or arm' any ship with intent, etc., etc." Since the act had never been tested in court, Hull drew up a hypothetical case without mentioning the Confederacy and submitted it to two eminent barristers, "both of whom filled the highest judicial positions." They concluded that it was no offense to equip a ship outside British territory or to equip a ship inside Great Britain if the ship did not intend to cruise against a friendly state. "The mere building of a ship within her Majesty's dominions by any person (subject or no subject) is no offence, whatever may be the intent of the parties, because the offence is not the building but the equipping." Hull used this decision to successfully argue that building a ship, without arming it in

British waters, did not violate the Foreign Enlistment Act. Throughout the war, he counseled Bulloch on every contract or important transaction. Bulloch described Hull as a "prudent, cautious, conscientious adviser" and a "watchful and safe mentor."[7]

Bulloch's efforts to maintain secrecy, however, met with almost immediate failure. Confederate agents, believing telegraph lines would not be monitored, identified Bulloch and accurately described his mission and his destination. Northern intelligence sources in Washington intercepted the message and New York newspapers published the details. Immediately after arriving in Liverpool, Bulloch to his dismay read the article spelling out his assignment, the names of his bankers, and the amount of money ($1 million) he had been allotted. Dudley, visiting England at this time, probably read the same article. Liverpool's acting consul, Henry Wilding, hired a private detective, Matthew Maguire, to learn if Bulloch was in Liverpool and to investigate all vessels shipping arms and munitions and all ships under construction. Wilding also alerted local authorities to be watchful for possible "privateering" activities; but he could not locate Bulloch until September 14.[8]

Despite this breach in security, Bulloch proceeded as if it had never occurred. The ideal commerce raider needed to be a wooden ship, capable of sailing under either steam or sail, with a large coal bunker for long periods at sea and a retractable propeller to reduce drag when under sail. After a quick inventory revealed no suitable vessels were available, Bulloch approached William C. Miller and Sons shipyard. Miller had been a shipwright for the Royal Navy and so had considerable experience in building wooden ships with berths for large crews and decks strong enough to carry heavy guns. Miller also had a scale drawing of a British gunboat that served as the basis for the *Florida's* design. Under Bulloch's direction, Miller stretched the design's midsection for greater speed and increased the carrying capacity by flattening the floor. Miller and Sons would build the hull and supply the masts, rigging, and so on. But since the Millers were not engineers, Bulloch contracted with Fawcett, Preston and Company for the engines. To conceal the true purpose and ownership of the vessel, he signed the contract in his own name as a private citizen and never openly discussed his connection with the Confederacy or revealed the ship's mission. Fawcett, Preston and Company carried the contract for construction of both the ship and its engines. To further thwart prying eyes and ears, the ship's dockyard name was the *Oreto* and she was rumored to be for a Palermo mercantile firm. Construction began within two weeks of Bulloch's arrival in Liverpool, although the first Confederate allocation did not reach England for another month, on July 27.[9]

Believing that personal supervision of the ship's construction was both unnecessary and unwise, Bulloch decided to return to the South to communicate directly with Secretary Mallory. He proposed buying a fast ship, loading it with badly needed military supplies, and sailing it into a Southern port. After his meeting with Mallory and other government officials, he would reload the ship with cotton and return to Liverpool. He met with local Confederate War Department representatives, who agreed to jointly finance the venture. Dudley Mann, the Confederate State Department emissary seeking British recognition of Southern independence, also endorsed the idea. Bulloch immediately bought the *Fingal*, a nearly new Scottish-built ship capable of steaming at thirteen knots. He placed her into a loading berth at Grennock and quickly sent the military supplies he had been accumulating. Again he operated in the utmost secrecy. Matthew Maguire had recently confirmed Bulloch's presence in Liverpool when his wife and children joined him in September. From then on Maguire or other operatives continually followed Bulloch and reported on his activities throughout the war.[10]

Maguire, however, lacked the skills and discretion one attributes to modern private detectives. Major Edward C. Anderson, another Confederate purchasing agent, easily spotted Maguire, who was tailing him. He described the detective as "an ugly, red headed villain whose faculties were by no means so acute as those of his metropolitan brother, and whose propensities for gazing innocently into the sky was remarkable." One night after visiting a friend, Anderson discovered Maguire on the friend's porch fast asleep, carefully stepped over his head, and continued on his way. Anderson, scheduled to return to the South on the *Fingal*, decided he would "make an emigrant" of Maguire if the detective followed him to Holyhead, from where he expected to embark. "My plan," Anderson recalled, "was to inveigle him on shipboard, put him in irons and convey him across the water to Dixie."[11] Fortunately for Maguire, he did not follow Anderson to Holyhead.

The *Fingal*, fully laden with fifteen thousand Enfield rifles, a million ball cartridges, two million percussion caps, sabers, revolvers, four heavy guns, and various other military supplies for the Confederate Army and Navy and the states of Georgia and Louisiana, arrived at Holyhead on October 15 to pick up Bulloch. As she slowly crept around the breakwater, in a heavy storm, she struck the Austrian brig *Siccardi* and sank her. Bulloch, upon learning of the disaster, quickly dressed, dashed off a note to Fraser, Trenholm and Company explaining the situation, boarded the *Fingal,* and ordered her to sail before customs officials could board and detain her. Fraser, Trenholm and Company notified the *Siccardi*'s owners and settled the loss through arbitration. The *Fingal* left immediately and after an uneventful voyage entered Savannah harbor on November 12. Although the Northern blockade strengthened as the war progressed, this increased the profits for those ships that successfully entered Southern ports. Southern and English captains, therefore, developed ships and tactics to improve their chances of eluding the Union blockaders. Carrying luxury items such as cigars, perfumes, and liquor, blockade runners generated 700 percent profits on each successful voyage, enough to pay for the ship and realize a profit after only two trips. Bulloch, after the war, remarked about the *Fingal*'s voyage, "No [other] single ship ever took into the Confederacy a cargo so entirely composed of military and naval supplies." His comment revealed one problem with the Confederacy's dependence upon privately owned blockade runners. They carried the most profitable items, not the ones most needed by the military.[12]

Wilding had learned where Bulloch lived and of his close connection with Fraser, Trenholm and Company, "whose office he visits daily." The vice consul reported the sailing of the *Fingal* and her cargo of "munitions of war for the Rebels" and several Southerners as passengers. Bulloch had left Liverpool a few days earlier, and Wilding speculated he might have joined the ship but would probably leave her in Ireland. Bulloch, however, was aboard the *Fingal* and, even then, sailing for Savannah. In any case, the vice consul hoped the *Fingal* "would be taken despite her English flag."[13]

So Bulloch was not in Liverpool when Dudley arrived on November 19, 1861. On the State Department's recommendation, the new consul retained Henry Wilding as vice consul. A British citizen who had served the consulate with "zeal and efficiency" since 1842, Wilding attended to much of the daily routine business of record keeping and assisting Americans abroad, leaving Dudley free for more pressing matters. In October Wilding had sent Maguire to investigate two suspicious ships: one in the Laird shipyard and the other in W. C. Miller and Sons' yard. The detective confirmed the ships' existence but learned little more. Since neither vessel would be complete and ready to sail immediately, Wilding did not press for more details. Dudley also kept Maguire, at Wilding's suggestion. Dudley even increased Maguire's pay from two pounds per week to three pounds one shilling per week, enough for an assistant detective. The new consul asked the State Department to pay the estimated $2,000 annual cost for detectives to combat Southern agents' activities purchasing war materials and "fitting out vessels for the so called southern Confederacy." The department declined. So Maguire's pay, as well as $4,000 in wages for Dudley's consulate staff, including Wilding, three clerks, and a messenger, came from the consulate's $7,500 annual budget, which included Dudley's salary.[14]

The *Trent* Affair and the possible resultant war occupied Dudley for his first several weeks in Liverpool. As the war frenzy gradually subsided in January 1862, he focused on the ships Wilding had noticed earlier. Dudley wrote Seward of the *"Oritis"* [sic], a "screw gun boat" built of iron and rumored for the Italian government. But because Fawcett and Preston, a company known to do business with the Confederacy, was building the engines, Dudley suspected the ship was meant for the South. He later noted that Fawcett and Preston had shipped "six thirty-two pound and one very large rifled cannon, a number of gun carriages and about sixty cases of shell & balls" to London. Dudley suspected these were the *Oritis's* guns and the ship would sail to "some out-port" to receive them.[15]

By February 4, 1862, Dudley had compiled new information, much coming from Maguire and other agents. The *Oreto* or *Oretis* was taking on coal and appeared ready to leave Liverpool within the week, without armament. She had "one funnel, three masts, bark rigged, eight port holes for guns on each side, and is to carry 16 guns." Although the builders were pretending the Italian government was the intended owner, the Italian consul denied any knowledge of the ship's ownership. The secrecy around the vessel had prevented Dudley from learning more details. He had written Minister Adams describing the *Oreto* and his conviction that she was a Confederate ship.[16]

A week later, on February 12, Dudley forwarded a more accurate and detailed description to Secretary Seward. The seven-hundred-ton *Oreto,* built by W. C. Miller and Sons and made of wood, was powered by both steam and sail. A lift with an iron chain hoisted the propeller to reduce drag while under sail. A drab paint job helped conceal her in dim light. She sported two "rakish" black chimneys with copper steam funnels and a brass cabin chimney. Three large drab-painted "shot boxes" were on each side, with seven others throughout the deck. She had two movable platforms near the larger ports for "long swivel guns," two more at the bow, and another two astern. The *Oreto* already had coal aboard and seemed ready to sail.[17] Dudley relayed the same information to Minister Adams.

Adams presented Dudley's evidence to Foreign Secretary Russell, including an extract from the letter describing the *Oreto,* but exaggerating her armament and claiming it was already aboard. This last bit of information, though erroneous, prompted Russell to begin an official inquiry. Despite the secrecy surrounding the *Oreto,* Dudley meanwhile discovered that Fraser, Trenholm and Company had advanced Fawcett, Preston and Company construction funds. This removed all doubt in Dudley's mind of the ship's ownership. He had also confirmed that Fawcett, Preston and Company had made the guns, and he surmised they would be mounted at sea to circumvent the

Foreign Enlistment Act. When fully armed, he believed this ship would be "quite equal in strength and armament to the [U.S. Navy warship] *Tuscarora*." She had made a trial trip the previous day [February 18] and was scheduled for another the next week. Again, he sent Minister Adams the latest information.[18]

Foreign Secretary Russell forwarded Adams's protest to the Lords of the Treasury and asked that they immediately investigate the matter. The Treasury passed the protest on to the Board of Customs, a Treasury subordinate agency, which directed it to Price Edwards, the Liverpool collector of customs. Edwards, who would later prove a staunch Confederate sympathizer, sent a customs officer to search the *Oreto* for armament. The officer reported that although the ship was pierced for guns there were neither guns nor gun carriages on board. Upon questioning, the ship's builders declared Thomas Brothers, a shipping company in Palermo, Italy, had contracted for the vessel and they presumed that was her destination. Based on this information, Edwards reported on February 21 that he believed Italians, not Confederates, owned the *Oreto*. The Board of Customs forwarded this report to Russell and he sent a copy on to Adams. Although Russell, still not satisfied, pursued the matter and tentatively learned the Italian government had no knowledge of the ship, he did not feel the foreign office should take immediate action to stop the *Oreto*.[19]

Dudley, meanwhile, had found a reliable informant aboard the vessel. William Parry, a British ship's pilot hired to guide the *Oreto* to sea, agreed to keep the consul apprised of her sailing preparations and possible true ownership, for a fee. He had received orders in strict secrecy to be ready, day or night, to set sail. Although their destination was reportedly Malta, Parry had "no doubt of her being for the Confd Gmt," and he expected she would not return from her next trial run. Three days later, on February 27, Parry wrote, "She is now victualed for a long cruise all her private stores are on board and filled up with coals. They are getting and trying to get as many Southern sailors as they possibly can so that they will remain with her."[20] He promised to telegraph additional information from any available port of call after the ship sailed. Parry also said the crew was only waiting for the West India mail steamer, due that day, before departing. Dudley again passed this latest news on to Seward and Adams on March 1 and added that a Scotsman named Dugnyd would initially captain and sail the *Oreto* from Liverpool as an English vessel. Dugnyd would take her on a trial run and not return. She would enter some port, perhaps the Isle of Man or Holyhead, take her guns on board, and then begin her cruise as a "privateer," a term Dudley often used to avoid giving any sense of legitimacy to the commerce raiders or to the Confederacy. Privateers were privately owned and operated and sailed under government-issued letters of marque granting them permission to raid enemy commerce in the government's name. The *Florida* and others were commerce raiders commissioned as Confederate vessels with a Confederate Navy captain in charge.[21]

Still, the ship did not sail. On March 5, Dudley informed Seward that the *Oreto* had registered as an English vessel, with W. C. Miller as her owner (this was inaccurate information) and Duguid (the correct spelling) as the captain. The crew was aboard, and Dudley enclosed a pay receipt he had purchased from one of the seamen showing Fawcett, Preston and Company had hired them. He had heard conflicting stories about where the guns would be taken aboard, one account said Palermo and another Bermuda. The ship had sailed the previous night, but Dudley had telegraphed consuls in Spanish, Portuguese, and Mediterranean ports to report any sightings. Two days later, the *Oreto* was back. Dudley admitted he was "quite unable to account for her conduct."[22]

Dudley's information, by this time, was remarkably accurate. The *Oreto* had been ready to put to sea for weeks. The delay was caused by a breakdown in communications during Bulloch's absence aboard the *Fingal* and a Confederate officer's indecision. Secretary Mallory had sent both Bulloch, a civilian representative, and James North, a Confederate naval officer, to England to purchase ships. The two often found themselves in conflict over money and their individual responsibilities. Before leaving for the South, Bulloch left clear instructions with Charles Prioleau, who had a detailed knowledge of the building contracts and funding, to deliver the *Oreto* to "any commissioned officer of the Confederate States Navy . . . who may be in England at the time," if Bulloch had not returned by the time the ship was ready to sail. Once he reached Savannah, however, Bulloch changed his mind. His trip had been so easy, he believed he could return to Liverpool before the *Oreto* was completed. He asked Mallory to assign him as the *Oreto*'s captain and to assign North to the second ship under construction (the *Alabama*). North received his revised orders in January 1862. In the meantime, the Northern blockade had strengthened, especially around Savannah, and Bulloch found himself unable to secure passage back to Liverpool. He asked Mallory to reverse the assignments and have North sail on the *Oreto*. Mallory complied, but unfortunately, North never received the revised orders.[23]

During Bulloch's absence, North leisurely visited several shipyards and occasionally checked on the progress of the *Oreto* and *290*, the builder's name for the *Alabama*. In early January, the *Oreto* was ready for launching and her trial runs, but North felt no responsibility to oversee preparations. After all, Bulloch had ignored him and made Prioleau responsible for the ship, and North had orders assigning him to the second vessel. On January 9, Prioleau asked North, as the senior Confederate naval officer present, to inspect the ship and take charge of her. Although North resisted, Prioleau persisted, showed him Bulloch's orders, and finally turned the ship over to him on February 5. Prioleau had even contacted Raphael Semmes, captain of the C.S.S. *Sumter* a makeshift commerce raider that Union ships had bottled up at Gibraltar, and offered him command of the *Oreto*. North considered taking temporary command himself and sailing her to Gibraltar. But Semmes told him not to bring her there, he would come get her. Semmes, however, became too busy with the *Sumter* and could not come to Liverpool. North did not want to take the ship to sea without orders from Mallory. He finally ordered the stores loaded and the crew aboard but pondered what to do next. Prioleau continued pressing North to get the ship away from Liverpool. The builders were well aware of Adams's complaint to Russell and they worried the Secretary would order the *Oreto* seized. Prioleau asked Major Caleb Huse, the Confederate Army purchasing agent, to intercede with North. Huse telegraphed North on February 21: "Immediate action necessary. . . . Ship will sail Tuesday [February 25]. Nothing can stop her but your positive orders."[24]

Although North initially seemed moved to take the *Oreto* out of England, he quickly decided to await Bulloch's return before acting. Perhaps North had learned of Price Edwards's report to the Board of Customs indicating the ship was intended for Italy and not the Confederacy. In any case, the *Oreto*, ready for sea and under suspicion, remained in Liverpool. Dudley watched her closely and kept Seward aware of her status. On February 26, 1862, he wrote, "The Oreto has not yet sailed. . . . Her guns will be smuggled on in some way. There is no doubt but what she is intended as a privateer for the Southern Confederacy," and a day later, "I have positive evidence that the Oreto gunboat is intended for the Southern Confederacy." On March 15, he informed Seward that Bulloch had returned.[25]

Bulloch had arrived back in Liverpool on March 10. In his account of events, he did not mention the confusion and controversy surrounding command of the *Oreto* or the delay getting her to sea. He found the ship fully provisioned, and Captain James Alexander Duguid and the crew, "engaged in strict conformity with the conditions of the Merchant Shipping Act," signing articles for a voyage to Palermo and ports in the Mediterranean or the West Indies. Bulloch thoroughly inspected the ship to ensure there was "not a single article of contraband of war" on board. "In this condition I was advised that according to the Municipal Law of Great Britain, she was a perfectly lawful article of traffic, that the builder could deliver her, and I could pay for and receive her, without infringing any statute, or transgressing any requirement of commercial property."[26]

Yet, the *Oreto* still did not sail. As she lay in the Mersey, Bulloch described her as a "comely craft, as much within her legal rights as a hundred cases of Birmingham rifles, or as many tons of gunpowder, about to start for New York in any other ship," which the British did not classify as exclusively war material. Even after Bulloch returned and assumed charge of the ship, there was no Confederate Navy captain readily available to take the *Oreto*'s helm. With the change in orders, Bulloch was to command the still unfinished second ship. He had assumed the *Nashville*'s captain, R. B. Pegram, and his staff would sail on the *Oreto*. Pegram was originally to provide Bulloch with "such officers to the *Oreto* as I might require," and Bulloch believed that with the change in circumstances Pegram would eagerly captain the commerce raider. Unfortunately, Pegram and the *Nashville* sailed before the new orders arrived.[27]

Knowing that Minister Adams would continue pressing the English government to detain the *Oreto*, Bulloch decided the ship should sail without her Confederate captain. Captain Duguid and the British crew would take her to the Bahamas. Bulloch expected Lieutenant John N. Maffitt, "a man of great natural resources—self-reliant, and fearless of responsibility," to be in Nassau. Maffitt was captaining blockade-runners between Nassau and Confederate ports and would be an ideal captain for the *Oreto*. Although Duguid was the ship's captain, Bulloch dispatched John Low, born in Liverpool but a resident of Savannah, as his special agent. Low had worked closely with Bulloch and had earned his complete confidence. Duguid was in charge at sea, but he was to follow Low's orders "as to movements and disposal of the ship" after they reached the "first port of destination." Bulloch warned Low that he must allow nothing to compromise the ship's character as a neutral vessel until after he had delivered her to a Confederate officer. Low was also responsible for all property aboard the ship. Upon reaching Nassau, he was to turn the *Oreto* and a letter of general sailing instructions over to Maffitt or any other Confederate naval officer and return immediately to Liverpool.[28]

The *Oreto* finally sailed from Liverpool on March 22, 1862, completely unarmed, under the British flag, commanded by a British captain, and manned by a British crew. Dudley continued gathering information, some accurate and some inaccurate, on the ship. The day she sailed, he wrote Seward that Bulloch would sail as captain and take her first to Madeira, then to Nassau, and finally into a Southern port. He admitted that the secrecy surrounding the ship had made it almost impossible to furnish reliable information about her, "notwithstanding the diligence used and effort made by me to obtain it. . . . They have managed this hushup better than anything else they have attempted at this port." Four days later he informed Seward that the *Oreto* had sailed directly for Bermuda and reported Bulloch was on board.[29]

After a rather uneventful voyage, the *Oreto* reached Nassau on April 28. The *Bahama*, which had sailed from Hartlepool about March 22 loaded with guns and ammunition, met her there. Lieutenant Maffitt, a twenty-eight-year veteran of the U.S. Navy, arrived aboard the blockade-runner *Gordon* on May 4. He found the *Oreto* "under a great cloud of suspicion . . . with her position daily becoming perilous and precarious." Dudley had earlier alerted U.S. consuls of the ship's nature and purpose, and the consul in Nassau had insisted that British authorities seize her for violating the Foreign Enlistment Act. The *Bahama* had been forced to transfer her cargo to a warehouse instead of directly to the *Oreto*. Although a British naval officer reported the ship "in every respect fitted as a man-of-war," a Nassau merchant who sympathized with the Confederacy testified that the *Oreto* was a commercial vessel. The British courts in Nassau freed the vessel. Maffitt later billed the Confederate Navy $248 for legal fees, "boat hire, bribes to the police and runners."[30]

After the courts released the *Oreto*, Captain Duguid moved her sixty miles to uninhabited Green Key, with Maffitt and eight officers as passengers. At Green Key, Maffitt spoke to the ship's English crew, explained the vessel's mission as a Confederate commerce raider, and invited them all to join him. Only thirteen agreed. This was truly bad news; he needed a crew of 140 officers and men. This began a period of such bad luck a suspicious man would have called the ship cursed. The legal delays in Nassau had taken nearly three months. By now it was August, and when the *Prince Albert* brought the *Oreto*'s armament from the storage warehouse, the meager crew transferred the heavy guns, shot, shells, powder, and stores in the broiling summer heat. When Maffitt inventoried his arms, he learned the rammers, sponges, sights, and firing locks for his six-inch guns had been forgotten in the warehouse. Then a crewman died, and the corpse bore a "yellow appearance," a sign of yellow fever. Maffitt pressed ahead and on the morning of August 17 called his crew together, read his orders of command, and commissioned the C.S.S. *Florida*. Meanwhile, in Liverpool, Dudley reflected that the local people expected "very soon to hear good news from her in the destruction of our ships—not the naval but those engaged in commerce."[31]

After trying in vain to add to his crew in Cuba and showing symptoms of yellow fever himself, Maffitt decided to put the *Florida* into a Confederate port. Having no pilot to guide a night run, he would have to make a dash into Mobile, Alabama, in daylight, through the blockading Union squadron, without functioning guns. Unable to stand unaided (one account had him tied in his chair), Maffitt ordered his remaining crew of eight officers and four seamen to replace the Confederate flag with British colors and clear the deck of everyone, except him and the helmsman. As the *Florida* approached the blockaders at fourteen knots, Commander George Preble of the U.S.S. *Oneida* assumed she was a British man-of-war checking the effectiveness of the blockade. He let the ship draw within one hundred yards before hailing her. When he received no answer, he fired across the bow. At that point, Maffitt hauled down the British flag, ran up the Confederate colors, and sped on toward safety. The four blockading Union ships opened fire, hitting the *Florida* several times but causing no vital damage. She broke through the blockade and into Mobile. It would be January 16, 1863, before a recovered Maffitt could gather a crew, repair his ship, and begin destroying Yankee merchant vessels.[32]

Adams and Dudley, meanwhile, continued building their case against the *Oreto*, now called the *Florida*, and the British government's responsibility in her escape. Adams sent Russell a second note in late March, protesting Britain's unfriendly attitude and ineffective neutrality laws. Russell replied that his country's laws were effective, if the accusers presented evidence of an offense. Although Russell did learn from his minister in Turin that the ship was not built for the Italian government, the news arrived on March 29, seven days after the *Oreto* had sailed. Dudley gathered sworn affidavits attesting to British complicity in the ship's construction and escape. This evidence, which he continued to compile, would eventually help sway the English government to reconsider shipbuilding for foreign belligerents and later convince an international tribunal that Great Britain should have been more diligent in enforcing her laws.[33]

After leaving Mobile in January 1863, Maffitt and the *Florida* and a series of tenders (captured ships later armed and commissioned as Confederate cruisers) burned Union merchant ships from the South Atlantic to Nova Scotia. Dudley closely monitored the ship's activities through newspaper reports and accounts from captains and crews of the *Florida*'s victims. He relayed any information, including rumors, on to the State and Navy Departments. On August 23, 1863, Maffitt guided his ship into Brest, France, for much needed repairs. Dudley at first believed the *Florida* would be escorting the ironclad rams nearing completion in England to sea, but he soon reported she was undergoing repairs at Brest. Captain and Mrs. Maffitt's presence in Dublin and the arrival of ninety crew members in Liverpool confirmed that the ship would be inactive for some weeks.[34]

Still suffering from his bout with yellow fever, Maffitt turned the *Florida* over to Lieutenant Charles Manifault Morris. As the repairs neared completion, Dudley feared the *Florida* and the C.S.S. *Georgia,* which was near Brest, would join in attacking the U.S.S. *Kearsarge* as she stood watch, hoping to prevent the *Florida*'s escape. But Morris, more interested in escaping than fighting, slipped back to sea on February 10, 1864. By then he found fewer Yankee merchant ships in the Atlantic. After several months at sea with few new captures, the *Florida* entered port at Bahia, Brazil, on the evening of October 4. The next morning, Morris discovered the U.S.S. *Wachusett* anchored nearby. Local officials met with Morris and the local U.S. consul, Thomas Wilson, and elicited promises to respect Brazil's neutrality. Commander Napoleon Collins, the *Wachusett*'s captain, however, could not resist the possibility of sinking the *Florida.* Waiting until 3 a.m. on October 7, when Morris and half his crew were ashore, Collins ordered his crew to ram the *Florida* and then board her. The *Wachusett,* under a full head of steam, struck the *Florida* on the starboard side, causing much damage. A boarding party then forced the ship's remaining crew to surrender. Although a Brazilian crew manning the fort guarding the harbor protected their country's honor by firing a perfunctory shot toward the *Wachusett*, Collins towed the *Florida* out of Bahia harbor and home to Hampton Roads, Virginia. Brazil, of course, protested this violation of international law and demanded the *Florida*'s return. The United States could not legally refuse, but on November 28, the army transport U.S.S. *Alliance* "accidentally" rammed and sunk the *Florida* as she lay at anchor at Hampton Roads. A court-martial board found Collins guilty of violating a neutral government's territorial jurisdiction and sentenced him to dismissal from the navy. Navy Secretary Gideon Welles, however, rejected the punishment, and Collins retired as a rear admiral in 1874.[35]

Meanwhile, by November 2 Dudley had received conflicting statements reporting the *Florida*'s capture either inside or outside Brazilian waters by the U.S.S. *Wisconsin*, the U.S.S. *Massachusetts* or the U.S.S. *Waychusets*. A week later, after receiving a more accurate accounting, he wrote Seward that the *Florida*'s fate had "blasted" the hopes of people in Liverpool, and "their grief is great and has broke out to raring for the outrage & wrong done to Brazil. They do not wait even for the facts or to hear what the persons have to say in justification." But he was undoubtedly glad "her career of burning and destroying" was ended.[36]

Despite her ignoble ending, the *Florida* had proved her worth as a commerce raider. She and her tenders captured sixty prizes, of which her crew burned forty-six and released thirteen others under a bond the ships' captains promised to pay the Confederate government at war's end. One other was recaptured by its crew. The sixty prizes totaled an estimated worth of over $4 million, or ten times the $400,000 cost to build and operate the *Florida*. Although Dudley followed the *Florida*'s activities through her cruise, with her sailing from Liverpool on March 22, 1862, his primary focus turned to the second vessel then under construction, the *290* in the Laird shipyard.[37]

THE *ALABAMA*

*The World's Most
Feared Commerce
Raider*

3

Failing to stop the *Oreto* (later known as the *Florida*), Dudley immediately shifted his focus with renewed determination to the *290*. He promised, "I shall . . . endeavor . . . in every way in my power to the full extent of my ability to thwart the emissaries and agents of the so called Southern Confederacy in their efforts to break to pieces and destroy our government."[1] Bulloch's second ship was also well under construction when Dudley arrived in November 1861. The previous June, while still negotiating with Miller and Sons for the *Oreto,* Bulloch visited Laird and Sons' Birkenhead shipyard, across the River Mersey from Liverpool. A tour of the facilities convinced him that the Lairds could build a ship suitable for commerce raiding. A few days later Bulloch returned and renewed the conversation. He explained he wished to build a wooden ship, powered by both sail and steam, with a retractable screw to reduce drag when she was under sail. After describing the vessel he wanted, Bulloch asked if the Lairds would calculate the specifications, make the drawings, and build a scale model on the assurance that he meant to do business. Bulloch agreed to pay £47,500 sterling (approximately $231,325) in five equal payments of £9,500 (approximately $46,265) each, the last payment to be made after the ship satisfactorily completed its trial runs and was delivered to him in Liverpool. The Lairds, unlike the Millers, waited until Bulloch's first funds arrived in late July and then signed the contract on August 1. They immediately began construction and the ship was to be ready to sail the following spring.[2]

This vessel, known during construction as the *290* since hers was the 290th hull laid down in the Laird shipyard, was larger than the *Florida*. Unlike her sister ship, which the Millers built following preexisting plans, the *290* included many of Bulloch's ideas and innovations. She was 210 feet long, as compared to the *Florida*'s 185 feet, and 1,024 tons versus 695 tons. Her breadth was 32 feet, her depth 17 feet 3 inches and maximum draft 15 feet. The *290* would have twin 300-horsepower engines that could drive her along at twelve knots. Like the *Florida,* she had a retracting propeller.[3]

The Lairds worked diligently on the ship, even during Bulloch's visit to the South in the fall of 1861. He later surmised that his absence might have increased the builders' determination to "turn out a first-class ship." Following Bulloch's instructions to use only the finest materials, the builders rejected two or three stern posts as unsuitable, even after they were bored for the propeller shaft. The final post cost £100 sterling, or nearly $500. The Lairds' conscientiousness, however, caused construction to progress more slowly than expected. While meeting with Confederate Navy Secretary Mallory, Bulloch asked for and was granted command of the *290*. Although disappointed that his ship was not ready to sail when he returned to Liverpool in March 1862, Bulloch was pleased with the workmanship. The *290* was "built of the very best materials, copper-fastened and coppered, and was finished in every respect as a first class ship." Since the Laird shipyard was more isolated than the Millers', he hoped to send the *290* to sea better prepared for her mission than the *Florida*. But the Lairds resisted, believing that even adding bolts for the broadside guns might be a violation of the Foreign Enlistment Act.[4]

Dudley undoubtedly learned of the *290*'s existence soon after arriving in Liverpool in November 1861, since Matthew Maguire had discovered her the previous month. Knowing the ship's launching was several months away, the new consul turned first to more pressing matters. The *Trent* Affair and the resultant war frenzy in England convinced him that his recall was imminent. As the war fear abated, Dudley dedicated himself to stopping the *Oreto*. With her escape, he was more determined than ever that the *290* would never prey on Northern shipping. Bulloch later acknowledged that the *Oreto*'s escape had "grieved and vexed" Dudley, and once the consul's suspicions were aroused, they kept his mind "in a wakeful and agitated condition during the remainder of the war."[5]

Gathering evidence in Liverpool's hostile environment proved difficult for Dudley. To make the task even harder, as he had with the *Oreto*, Bulloch contracted for the *290* in his own name, as a private individual. Dudley later explained to Secretary of State Seward there were only two ways to obtain evidence—persuasion and bribery. Persuading a local worker to provide information important to the North was virtually impossible. Paying a bribe tainted the evidence and made it nearly useless in court. Although Dudley considered detectives in general not "very esteemable men," he felt compelled to rely even more heavily on Maguire and his associates. Since their business was "not a very pleasant one," the consul had to pay them well and cover their travel expenses when he sent them out of town to pursue leads elsewhere. Dudley spent $1,268.82 trying to stop the *290,* and this money came from his own pocket since the State Department did not begin reimbursing him for this cost until 1863. The consul later fired Maguire for padding his expense account and lying in his reports as a means of increasing his income.[6]

By March 1, 1862, Dudley began to report regularly on the gunboat in the Laird shipyard, which he believed was intended for the South. Within a month, information gleaned from various sources suggested this was an exact model of the *Oreto*. Soon crew members from the *Sumter*—the makeshift raider Captain Rafael Semmes had launched and sailed with limited success, but which was now bottled-up at Gibraltar—arrived in Liverpool and bragged that the vessel in the Laird yard was only one of several the English were building for the Confederacy. The crew also indicated that Captain Semmes would soon command a steam-powered man-of-war under construction at Silloth. Dudley dispatched a man to Silloth, but he could find nothing. This was only one of several false rumors he pursued during the war. But he remained convinced a vessel was being built for Semmes and the one in Laird yard was probably it. Semmes himself spent a few weeks in Liverpool before leaving for the South.[7]

Henry Laird, one of the brothers building the ship, meanwhile informed a British Army officer that the Spanish government owned *290*. Dudley heard the rumor and suggested that Minister Adams check with the Spanish minister in London. Adams agreed and sent Benjamin Moran, his assistant secretary, to inquire at the Spanish legation. The Spanish denied any knowledge of the ship, thereby confirming to Dudley that she was bound for the Confederacy.[8]

On May 14, 1862, the Lairds launched the *290*. Hoping to quiet the suspicions already aroused, Bulloch had her christened the *Enrica*, the Hispanicized version of the christener's given name, possibly his wife, Harriet. He later refused to identify the lady, saying only, "She graciously consented to perform the office, and fulfilled it in a comely manner, little knowing that she was constructively taking part in a great Civil War." Workmen still called the ship the *290*, and they immediately warped her into position and placed her over the blocks. The "Great Derrick" swung out from an adjacent dock and began placing the first of her heavy machinery aboard even before she was secured in her berth. Within three days, all her engines and boilers were in place. Work on the *Enrica* progressed quickly. Soon after the launching, Lieutenant John Hamilton, slated as Bulloch's executive officer, arrived and helped with completing the ship and drilling her crew.[9]

Dudley reported the *Enrica*'s launching to Seward and included a more detailed description, which he had obtained from workers in the shipyard, including "one of the leading workmen" and the foreman. Her contract specified that she be of the finest materials and in the "best & finest manner with no regard to expence." Her timbers were the "very best English Oak, every plank & timber was most critically examined." Workmen caulked every plank as it went on and fastened everything with copper bolts. According to the foreman overseeing the construction, "no boat was ever built stronger or better than her." Dudley had no doubt "but what she is intended for the Rebels."[10]

A month later, on June 15, the ship made her first trial run. Her performance pleased Bulloch. She still needed additional equipment, sailing supplies, a crew, and her officers before she would be ready for sea duty. Bulloch, well aware that Federal "spies were lurking about" and that "a detective named Maguire was taking a deep and abiding interest" in his movements, limited public access to the trial run. Dudley reported that no one, including the press, was allowed on board during the run, except "persons actively engaged in aiding the Rebellion." He believed that articles published in the New York newspapers about Liverpool's shipbuilding activities caused Bulloch to be more cautious, which made gathering evidence against the *Enrica* more difficult. Nevertheless he had learned her hull was black with a red shield painted on the billet head and she had three bark-rigged masts—all square-rigged except the after mast, which was fore-and-aft rigged. Her screw propeller retracted while she was under sail and she "was calculated to run fifteen knots per hour." He concluded, "No pains or expense has been spared in her construction. And when finished will be a very superior boat of her class. Indeed they say there will be no better afloat."[11]

As the ship neared completion, she needed a Board of Trade certified captain to prepare her for sea and hire a crew. Bulloch sought a man with "professional competency, prudence, control over the tongue, and absolute integrity." A friend directed him to Captain Mathew J. Butcher, a first officer on a Cunard steamship. The two men had met three years earlier in Havana. A brief conversation convinced Bulloch that Butcher had the desired traits to captain the *Enrica*. Bulloch explained that Butcher was to oversee the outfitting of the vessel and captain her to a port outside England. The crew must be enlisted simply to sail her to the West Indies, none were to be engaged for Confederate service. Also the ship would be totally unarmed. The two men quickly reached an "understanding." Bulloch then introduced Butcher to the Lairds and informed them that the new captain would relay all instructions on outfitting the ship. Bulloch later praised Butcher for completing his duties "not only with tact, judgment and discretion, but with the nice and discriminating fidelity which marks the man of true honesty."[12]

The *Enrica* was so nearly complete by July 1 that Bulloch ordered Lieutenant John Low, who had helped deliver the *Florida,* aboard as first officer. Bulloch then hired master's mate George Townley Fullam as second officer, surgeon David H. Llewellyn, paymaster Clarence R. Yonge (a Confederate seaman whom Bulloch had met in Savannah, Georgia, the previous autumn and who had accompanied him back to Liverpool in March), and J. McNair, the *Fingal's* engineer, as chief engineer. All were British citizens, except Yonge. First Lieutenant Hamilton and Captain Butcher, the remaining officers, made final preparations. Bulloch packed and arranged his personal affairs in anticipation of commanding the ship on her commerce-raiding mission. Since Secretary Mallory left him great discretion in his operating instructions, Bulloch proposed rendezvousing with Captain Maffitt and the *Florida* and making "a joint dash at a given point." Ready to sail within the week, he received two letters that "greatly disappointed [his] hopes and expectations in reference to getting afloat."[13]

The first message, from Secretary Mallory, said he had ordered Captain Rafael Semmes, the former captain of the C.S.S. *Sumter* and the South's first commerce raider, back to England to command the *Enrica.* Mallory explained that Bulloch's experience made his continued service in Liverpool absolutely essential. The secretary directed him, if possible, to build two more raiders like the *Enrica* and, more important, to explore the building of ironclad vessels, ships that could sink the Union's wooden blockaders with impunity. Mallory had discussed this option with Bulloch during his recent visit to the South. In the second letter, Semmes wrote that he would return from Nassau by the first available ship and asked that Bulloch complete the *Enrica's* preparations for sea. Lieutenant Hamilton would not sail as executive officer since Semmes brought his own officers. Instead, Hamilton stayed in Liverpool and assisted Bulloch.[14]

To have to wait for Semmes to arrive created a dilemma for Bulloch since the ship already had all her stores and a full load of coal on board. She was ready to sail by the middle of July, needing only to fill out her crew. He hesitated to hire the crew too early lest they attract notice with their "loose talk." In accordance with Bulloch's strict orders, there were no weapons of any kind aboard. As with the *Florida,* her armament would ship separately. Shortly after the Lairds began construction, Bulloch had contracted with various manufacturers for the *290's* guns, munitions, personal weapons, uniforms, and stores for a 150-man crew. He directed each vendor to complete his order, then pack it and await shipping instructions. Near the end of May, a "suitable agent" purchased the *Agrippina,* a moderate-size ship, and loaded her with 350 tons of coal. By July the merchants had shipped the *Enrica's* armament and stores and the *Agrippina's* crew had everything on board. She loaded in London and no one connected her to the *Enrica.* She had cleared customs for Guyana and only awaited word from Bulloch. Bulloch considered the situation critical, as he knew Dudley and Adams were pressing the British to seize the *Enrica,* and each day's delay improved their chances of success.[15]

Dudley, meanwhile, was convinced that the Lairds were building the *Enrica* for the South and wrote Minister Adams detailing his reasons for believing she was destined to be a commerce raider. Two officers from the C.S.S. *Sumter* had admitted Southern ownership of the vessel. The Lairds' foreman called her the sister ship of the *Oreto* and claimed she was built for the same purpose. When pressed to explain further, the foreman stated that she would be a "privateer" for the "Southern Government of the United States." The captain and officers of the *Julie Usher,* engaged in trade with the South and "loaded to run the blockade," stated this was a Confederate ship and Bulloch was to be her captain. To Dudley this evidence was "entirely conclusive." After describing the vessel in detail, he told Adams that "she will be a most formidable and dangerous craft and if not prevented from going to sea will do much mischief to our commerce." He then quoted her builders who said "no better vessel of her class was ever built." Believing the ship could sail within ten days, Dudley personally delivered his note to Adams in London.[16]

The *Julie Usher* also produced another information source, a young Southern boy named Robinson whose parents had apparently sent him to England to live with a guardian and attend school there. Homesick, Robinson ran away from school and sailed for the South on the blockade-runner *Julie Usher*. For some unexplained reason the ship returned to Liverpool without completing her crossing and Robinson's guardian recovered him. Henry Wilding, Dudley's deputy, learned of these events and sent Maguire to talk with the guardian and the boy. Concerned he would flee again, the guardian hired Maguire to watch over the boy until he could be enrolled at Stoneyhurst College. The boy lived at Maguire's house for about two weeks, never knowing the detective worked for the Union consul in Liverpool.[17]

Finding a confidant in Maguire, Robinson shared information he had overheard while aboard the *Julie Usher*, including a conversation about the ship under construction in the Laird yard. A Southern ship, she would carry eleven guns and would sail in about eleven days, under Bulloch's command. According to what the boy had learned, Bulloch would not enter a Confederate port but would immediately start raiding Northern commerce. Robinson told Maguire that Fraser, Trenholm and Company had advanced the money for this new ship. The boy pleaded with his new friend to intercede with Bulloch to get him a berth on the *Enrica*. With Dudley in London conferring with Adams, Wilding asked Maguire to find "some shrewd and likely man" to visit Bulloch and solicit a position for the boy. Wilding thought the scheme worth a try but believed Bulloch was "too knowing" to "fall into the trap." Apparently this assessment proved correct as the boy did not sail with the *Enrica*. Wilding then tried to obtain an affidavit from Robinson, but the boy refused.[18]

Dudley and Wilding both concluded that Robinson's testimony would convince Liverpool customs official Price Edwards to seize the *Enrica*. So they each wrote Edwards recounting their case, including this damning evidence from Robinson. Since he was already in London, Dudley submitted the letters to Adams for his approval before mailing them. Adams asked Dudley not to send the letters to Edwards, but instead to write Adams outlining the case. As Dudley later explained to Secretary Seward, Adams believed the British government officials' attitude toward the United States had improved and that they would "do what they can to conciliate us, and will stop the fitting out of this vessel." Dudley presented his evidence to Minister Adams on June 21, and Adams passed it on with an "energetic note" to Foreign Secretary Lord Russell asking him to either stop the ship or to "establish the fact that its purpose is not inimical to the people of the United States." Dudley prayed the British would stop the ship but had little confidence they would do so. Adams, meanwhile, ordered the U.S.S. *Tuscarora* to move from its normal duty station near Spain to Southampton. If the *Enrica* escaped, he would authorize the *Tuscarora* to intercept her. Dudley hoped this would happen and again expressed concern for the damage the *Enrica* could do to Northern commerce. The ship was ready to "enter upon the business as a Privateer at once" without entering a Southern port. He repeated to Seward that Bulloch would be the ship's commander.[19]

Lord Russell, still holding to the opinion that the U.S. representatives were responsible for proving a violation of the Foreign Enlistment Act, forwarded Adams's and Dudley's letters to the law officers of the Crown and the Lords Commissioners of the Treasury for their opinion on the evidence. The law officers, consisting of the attorney general, the solicitor general, and the queen's advocate, advised on legal questions of great national interest, while the Lords Commissioners oversaw the entire customs services. The law officers informed Russell that if Adams's and Dudley's claims were true, the building and equipping of the *Enrica* violated the Foreign Enlistment Act and Russell should prevent the ship from sailing. They recommended that the government direct customs authorities at Liverpool to investigate the Union charges in order to learn the truth. The Treasury officials, on the other hand, reported that customs officials had already investigated the ship and determined it was a warship, but since the builders refused to disclose its destination there were no grounds for detaining her. The customs officials recommended that Dudley present his evidence to Price Edwards at Liverpool, who would then decide if it were sufficient to require action. Russell's choice was either to follow the law officers' suggestion and order British officials to investigate and prove or disprove the charges or to continue requiring that Dudley and Adams gather the evidence for the British customs officials to evaluate. Russell decided to pursue his previous course, which was the same one the customs officials supported, and placed the burden of proof again on Dudley. Russell replied to Adams's letter on July 4 suggesting that Dudley submit his evidence, consisting of signed affidavits, to the Liverpool collector of customs. Adams immediately directed Dudley to comply with Russell's recommendation.[20]

Adams's instructions to Dudley on July 8 caused the consul some consternation. He relied heavily on information gathered by Maguire and his associates and statements from workers and others knowledgeable about the nature of the *Enrica*. This "evidence" by today's standards was mere hearsay. To further complicate the matter, Dudley had promised not to reveal the workers' names; to do so would not only violate the trust they placed in him but also ensure they would never work in Liverpool's shipyards again. Also, if he disclosed the detectives' identities, they would be of little further use to him. In his letter to Edwards on July 9, Dudley chose to build his case without revealing his sources. He related to the collector of customs "information and circumstances" that had "come to [his] knowledge" about the "gunboat being fitted out by Messrs Laird at Birkenhead for the Confederates of the Southern United States of America and intended to be used as a Privateer against the United States." The vice consul and "others" had told him of the *Oreto* and this ship upon his arrival in Liverpool. The *Oreto* sailed in March and was now in Nassau, where she was receiving her armament and preparing to begin raiding U.S. merchant ships. His attention had repeatedly been called to the *Enrica* by "various persons who stated that she also was for a Confederate privateer." Two officers from the "Privateer *Sumter*," while passing through Liverpool, had stated the gunboat building in the Laird shipyard was for the Confederacy. One of the Laird foremen had described the *Enrica* as the *Oreto*'s sister ship, intended for the same purpose. Bulloch and other "well known agents of the Confederate Government" had been present at the ship's various trials. Dudley also recounted the Robinson boy's story about the gunboat. He then concluded he had "formed an undoubting conviction" that this ship was intended as a Confederate vessel that would prey on Union shipping. His information had come from "a variety of sources," many of whom had furnished it "out of friendly regard for the United States in strict confidence," and he could not "furnish their names." He concluded, "My information satisfies me beyond a doubt that she is intended for a Confederate war vessel."[21]

Edwards acknowledged receipt of Dudley's letter and passed it on to the Board of Customs. He expressed doubt, however, that the board would act unless Dudley produced evidence to "legally substantiate" his statements. On July 16, Edwards informed Dudley that the customs commissioners' solicitor, F. J. Hammel, did not believe his "details" legally justified customs' detaining the ship. If customs officials stopped a ship and could not prove in court that it had violated the law, the British government had to pay the ship's owner all court costs and lost income, which could be substantial.[22]

Dudley expressed his outrage in a letter to Adams. From his perspective, when American officials notified the British government that an English firm was building a Confederate ship to raid U.S. commerce vessels, British officials should intercede and investigate the charges. Price Edwards's response indicated that Americans must produce evidence equivalent to that required in a "court of Justice." If this indeed were the case, Dudley felt it was "hardly worth spending our time in making further application to them." Adams, however, believed that if the situation were reversed, Americans would require the same level of proof and suggested that Dudley support his case with affidavits from his sources. It is interesting that Adams, the diplomat, was suggesting Dudley, the attorney, build his case on more solid evidence.[23]

After the Board of Customs officially denied Dudley's request, Adams, irritated that Dudley had not submitted the signed affidavits as the minister originally suggested, directed the consul to hire a solicitor and compile the necessary affidavits. Dudley hired A. T. Squarey, a Liverpool attorney whom he often relied upon, and began contacting those who had given him information. As he expected, some with detailed knowledge refused to give affidavits. The Robinson boy, for example, readily talked with Maguire but would not sign or swear to a written statement. Dudley collected affidavits from William Passmore, a British seaman; John Da Costa, a British shipping master; A. S. Clare, a private citizen; Maguire, the private detective; and Wilding, the vice consul.[24]

Dudley and Squarey presented their witnesses to Price Edwards on July 21 and had them swear to their affidavits before him. Dudley also submitted a statement, but since his Quaker beliefs prohibited swearing on the Bible he simply affirmed its veracity. Squarey explained to Edwards the nature of the case, the applicable parts of the Foreign Enlistment Act, and the urgency for action. The solicitor then formally applied to have the *Enrica* seized for violating the act. Edwards replied that he must refer the matter to the Board of Customs for direction.[25]

Dudley and Squarey immediately left for London to consult with Adams and bring him copies of these affidavits. Adams forwarded the documents to the Foreign Office and suggested Dudley and Squarey consult with Queen's Counsel H. R. Collier, an esteemed barrister, for his opinion. Wilding, meanwhile, had found two more witnesses: Robert Taylor, a Confederate seaman who made his statement without realizing it would be used against the *Enrica*, and Edward Roberts, a ship's carpenter. The vice consul quickly sent these affidavits to Dudley in London. Squarey presented the additional evidence directly to Hammel and learned then that the board deemed the first six affidavits insufficient to warrant action.[26]

Unbeknownst to Dudley or Squarey, the Board of Customs as a matter of course notified the Lords Commission of Her Majesty's Treasury of its finding on the affidavits. The Lords of the Treasury now believed the United States might indeed have a case, so they wrote an unofficial letter to Foreign Office Undersecretary Austen Henry Layard asking if Lord Russell wanted the law officers consulted. Russell immediately suggested they

President Abraham Lincoln—President Lincoln's blockade closed the Southern ports to legitimate foreign trade and prompted the South to look to England for ships. The National Archives

Secretary of State William S. Seward—State Secretary Seward's threat to provoke a foreign war to reunite the country probably made British officials more cautious when dealing with Confederate emissaries. The National Archives

Minister to Great Britain, Charles Francis Adams—Perfectly suited in temperament and background for his position, Minister Adams presented Dudley's evidence of Confederate shipbuilding to the British government. National Park Service, Adams National Historical Park

above—**Confederate agent James Bulloch**—The South's most trusted and able agent in Europe, Bulloch's determination to build a Confederate Navy rivaled Dudley's dedication to preventing it. The Naval Historical Foundation

left—**Confederate Navy Secretary Stephen Mallory**—Secretary Mallory believed a small fleet incorporating the latest technological advances could rival a Northern navy of vastly superior numbers. The National Archives

C.S.S. *Florida*—After a nearly disastrous beginning, the *Florida* proved to be an excellent commerce raider. The Naval Historical Foundation

John Maffitt, captain of the C.S.S. *Florida*—Captain Maffitt's extraordinary courage saved his ship and made her a scourge for the Northern merchant fleet. The Library of Congress

Raphael Semmes, captain of the C.S.S. *Alabama*—Seemingly operating with impunity, Captain Semmes nearly cleared the seas of Northern shipping. His large waxed moustache added to the dashing image that raised Semmes and the *Alabama* to legendary status and made them welcome guests in ports around the world. The Library of Congress

C.S.S. *Alabama*—The *Alabama,* the most feared commerce raider in history, captured more than sixty Union merchant ships and caused hundreds of others to change registry to avoid the same fate. Reproduced by permission of the Huntington Library, San Marino, California

56

The *Alexandra*—The *Alexandra* earned her place in history not on the seas but in the courts as the first test case for the British Foreign Enlistment Act. Reproduced by permission of the Huntington Library, San Marino, California

above—**H.M.S.** *Wyvern* (called *El Monassir* while under construction to disguise her ownership)—Originally built for the Confederacy by Laird and Sons, this ironclad included the five great naval innovations of the mid-nineteenth century and promised to be an unstoppable weapon that could destroy the Northern blockading vessels and lay siege to Northern coastal cities. Reproduced by permission of the Huntington Library, San Marino, California

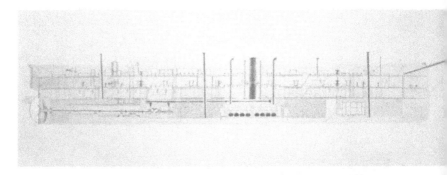

above—The *Danmark* (cutaway view)—James North believed this would be the ship that would break the Northern blockade. This cutaway shows the engines well protected within the ship's armor plating and the ample space to accommodate a large crew. Reproduced by permission of the Huntington Library, San Marino, California

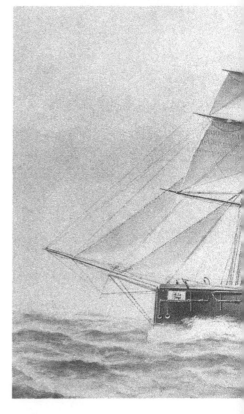

The *Danmark*—Built by Thomson Brothers for the Confederacy, this ironclad was considerably larger than the Laird rams and, therefore, appeared to be even more formidable. Reproduced by permission of the Huntington Library, San Marino, California

C.S.S. *Shenandoah*—Captained by James Waddell, the *Shenandoah* effectively destroyed the Northern whaling fleet. Sailing in Arctic waters where news of Confederate defeat did not reach her until August 1865, the *Shenandoah* did her greatest damage after General Robert E. Lee's surrender at Appomattox in April 1865. Reproduced by permission of the Huntington Library, San Marino, California should do so, and the Lords of the Treasury forwarded Dudley's package on to the queen's law officers, requesting an opinion "at their earliest convenience."[27]

Discouraged by the Board of Customs' apparent refusal to act, Dudley and Squarey returned to consult with Collier. The queen's counsel, after reviewing the affidavits, responded, "It appears difficult to make out a stronger case of infringement of the Foreign Enlistment Act which if not enforced on this occasion is little better than a dead letter." He concluded that the U.S. government would have "serious grounds for remonstrance" if the British officials allowed the *Enrica* to escape. Squarey then submitted the two new affidavits and a copy of Collier's opinion to the Board of Customs and asked that it reconsider its opinion based on this new information. Hammel, the board's solicitor, did not believe the additional affidavits strengthened the Americans' case and disagreed with Collier's opinion. Hammel's regard for Collier's reputation, however, prompted him to forward the package on to the Lords of the Treasury with a recommendation they pass it on to the law officers. The documents reached the solicitor at 3:45 in the afternoon of July 23, and by 5:30 he had sent them on to the Treasury officials.[28]

Dudley insisted that Squarey also personally deliver this additional evidence to the Foreign Office. Squarey, "with some difficulty," obtained an interview with Undersecretary Layard. Although Layard was reluctant to act, Squarey impressed upon him "the extreme urgency of the matter" and "the danger in delay." Layard sent Russell a note inquiring if he should send the package to the law officers "at once," and Russell replied, "Yes, at once." Layard delivered the affidavits on that same evening. So by the evening of July 23, the law officers had eight of nine affidavits attesting to the *Enrica*'s character, ownership, and purpose.[29]

The following day, Squarey delivered one more affidavit, from Henry Redden who claimed to be the boatswain aboard the *Enrica,* to the Board of Customs. Squarey then learned that the board had forwarded the previous package to the Lords of the Treasury for their advice. The next day the board sent this ninth affidavit to the Treasury who relayed it to the law officers. The board also informed Squarey that the Treasury commission had referred the case to the Crown's law officers. Squarey, satisfied he had done his best, left for Liverpool.[30]

Having done all he could in London, Dudley had returned to Liverpool the day before. Determined to aid in the *Enrica*'s capture if she managed to escape, he hired a photographer to take a picture of the ship, to be distributed to U.S. Navy ships. Unfortunately, she lay among other vessels and the photographer's efforts failed. The consul also attempted to hire John Higinson, a local seaman, to sail on the ship. As Dudley explained to Seward, Higinson would be a valuable witness if a Union captain could stop and capture the ship. Although Dudley could not reach an agreement with Higinson, the consul believed John Readdy, a New Englander who did sail on the Confederate ship, "could be procured as a witness."[31]

Dudley wrote Seward that while he hoped for the best he was "quite prepared for the worst." He had done all he could to stop the *Enrica* from sailing, more than he felt any government should require another friendly nation to do. Both Squarey and Collier believed the evidence was not only strong enough to have the vessel detained but sufficient to have her condemned in any court.[32]

On Saturday, July 26, two days after Squarey presented his final affidavit to the Board of Customs, the entire package reached the desk of Sir John Harding, the queen's counsel. Unfortunately, at about this same time, Harding suffered what Foreign Secretary Russell later called "symptoms of the brain," possibly a stroke. Harding's wife concealed her husband's condition for two days. Not until Monday, July 28, did Attorney General William Atherton see the documents. After reviewing the case against the *Enrica* and considering Collier's opinion, Atherton felt the government should stop the ship from sailing. But he wanted to consult with Solicitor General Roundell Palmer, the third of the law officers, before issuing an opinion. Atherton and Palmer met that evening and agreed the ship should be seized. They relayed their decision to Russell the next morning, July 29.[33]

The law officers explained that the *Enrica*'s construction defined her as a warship and the four sailors' testimony indicated she was destined for the Confederate States to be used against the United States. They acknowledged she had no armament aboard but believed the Foreign Enlistment Act should be interpreted to include "construction" as well as "equip, furnish, fit out, or arm." To apply the narrower definition would "fritter away the act, and give impunity to open and flagrant violations of its provisions." The attorney and solicitor generals recommended that, "without loss of time, the vessel be seized by the proper authorities."[34]

Bulloch, meanwhile, was well aware of the efforts to stop the ship. A "private but most reliable source" had informed the Confederate agent on July 26 that "it would not be safe to leave the ship in Liverpool another forty-eight hours." Bulloch never identified his source, although he later hinted the information came through his solicitor, "who managed to find out the particulars of some of [Dudley's] affidavits." He denied that any British official had conveyed any information directly to him and that he had bribed anyone for it. Word of the ship's impending seizure came "not by any treachery or breach of trust, but in a very simple, regular, and ordinary way."[35] Although there is no remaining evidence identifying Bulloch's source, it is interesting to note that Price Edwards and Bulloch shared the same solicitor and Edwards speculated heavily in Southern cotton. Edwards's later actions seem to support the suspicion that he might have been the source.[36]

After receiving the warning, Bulloch told the Lairds he wanted another all-day sea trial for the *Enrica*. The Lairds had previously agreed to take her out again if Bulloch requested it, although she had already completed the required trials. He confidentially alerted Captain Butcher to load extra coal and complete his stores as the ship would not return after the trial. Bulloch also directed John Low, who had returned from delivering the *Florida*, and Clarence Yonge to sail with the *Enrica*. Bulloch cautioned Yonge not to reveal his connection with the Confederate Navy, but to mingle with the crew and encourage them to stay with the ship for her commerce-raiding voyage.[37]

On Monday, July 28, 1862, the ship came out of dock and anchored nearby. Her coal and supplies were on board, a $100,000 cruising fund was on hand, and she lacked only the remainder of her crew to be ready for sea. The next morning at about 9 o'clock, draped in flags, with Bulloch and several civilians including women and Laird employees aboard creating a festive atmosphere, the *Enrica* cast off for a "trial run." The tug *Hercules* accompanied her as tender. After several runs, during which the *Enrica* averaged nearly thirteen knots, Bulloch explained to his guests that he wished to keep the ship out overnight for additional trials and asked them to return with him to Liverpool on the *Hercules*. He confidentially directed Butcher to take the ship to Moelfra Bay, on the coast of Wales, and wait for him there. Bulloch and his guests boarded the *Hercules* at about 4 p.m. and sailed back to Liverpool. While on board, he arranged for the tug to meet him at 6 o'clock the following morning, telling the ship's master that he wished to take a few items out to the *Enrica*. Bulloch had previously contracted with a shipping master for thirty to forty men, willing to ship to the Bahamas or some other port, to meet him at the loading dock at that time.

Bulloch met the *Hercules* at about 7 a.m. on July 30. She already had the needed equipment and spares on board. They did not include gunpowder, as Dudley's agents would report, but spare anchor stock, material for a frame for the extra spars, and additional brass fittings for the engines. Also awaiting Bulloch were between thirty-five and forty men and nearly as many women of the "class who generally affect a tender solicitude for Jack when he is outward-bound, and is likely to be provided with an advance-note." He directed the shipping master to get the men aboard, but of course the women could not go. To which, the shipping master replied it was "all or none." The women expected to collect the men's first month's pay and would not leave until they got it. The men would not go without the women accompanying them to the ship. Knowing he could not afford a delay, Bulloch reluctantly relented and hurried everyone on board. He was concerned not only with the threat of seizure by British customs, but "a judicious friend at

Southampton" had telegraphed him that the U.S.S. *Tuscarora* had left there and was probably headed for Queenstown to intercept the *Enrica*.

The *Hercules* reached Moelfra Bay and the *Enrica* at about 3 o'clock in the afternoon of July 30. It had rained earlier and a real storm was blowing in. By then, with nothing to eat on board the *Hercules*, "Jack and his fair friends were therefore hungry, and not in suitable frame of mind for business." Bulloch ordered the *Enrica*'s steward to prepare a "substantial supper as quickly as possible." After all had eaten a hearty meal, a "safe allowance of grog, to add zest and cheerfulness to the meal," and a "pipe," Bulloch explained to the men that the ship had satisfactorily completed her trials and he proposed sending her on a voyage to Havana, "touching at any intermediate port." He offered one month's pay in advance and free passage back to Liverpool if the ship did not return. All but two or three men agreed to go, and each man "with his lady" came to the cabin in turn, signed the agreement, collected his advance pay, which he promptly turned over to his companion. It was nearly midnight before the new crew members completed their transactions and by then heavy rain was coming down in "spiteful squalls." Even though Bulloch considered it "inhospitable to turn the ladies out on such a night," there were no accommodations for the women on board the *Enrica*. They, therefore, boarded the *Hercules* and returned to Liverpool.

The law officers' recommendation for seizure, meanwhile, worked its way back through official channels. The response moved much more deliberately than the original inquiry. The Foreign Office received the officers' opinion on July 29 but did not forward it on to the Lords of the Treasury until July 30. Another day passed before Treasury directed the Board of Customs to seize the *Enrica*. Not until July 31 did the board telegraph customs officials at Liverpool and Cork to act, if the vessel was in their port. The board sent a similar message to Beaumaris and Holyhead on August 1 and another to Cork the following day to retain her if she put in to Queenstown. By this time, the *Enrica* was in neither port. Years later William Titherington, an acquaintance of Price Edwards, recounted in an affidavit that he told Edwards a few days later that local newspapers blamed him for the *Enrica*'s escape. According to Titherington, Edwards replied, "My dear boy how could I prevent it, for I was out of the way, at the very top of the pool when she sailed." Titherington interpreted Edwards's remark to mean that the collector was purposely beyond reach so he could not have been available to stop the ship even if the telegram had arrived in time.[38]

Bulloch remained aboard the *Enrica* to ensure she reached the Atlantic safely. Anticipating that the *Tuscarora* would try to block the usual route south, he directed Captain Butcher to sail north around Ireland. George Bond, the pilot Bulloch had brought with him on the *Hercules,* and Butcher agreed this was best. Shortly after midnight the storm hit with strong winds and heavy rain. Despite the weather, Bulloch felt circumstances dictated they move immediately. The *Enrica* weighed anchor about 2:30 a.m. on July 31. The wind and rain soon abated and she averaged thirteen knots throughout the day. About six o'clock that evening, the *Enrica* hailed a fishing boat off the Giants' Causeway in Northern Ireland, and Bulloch and Bond went aboard. Before leaving, Bulloch instructed Butcher to take his ship to Terceira, the beautiful little bay in the Azores that Bulloch had spotted the previous October when the *Fingal* had been forced to enter port to replenish its water supply. Butcher was to meet the *Agrippina* there. Captain Semmes would soon join him there to take command of the *Enrica.* Butcher proceeded to sea while Bulloch and Bond spent the evening in a local hotel before returning to Liverpool by train on August 1. When Bulloch reached Liverpool he learned the *Agrippina* had already sailed with her cargo to meet the *Enrica.*[39]

Even after the *Enrica* sailed on July 29, Dudley still hoped the British would stop her before she escaped to international waters. That evening one of Dudley's men reported that the tug *Hercules* had loaded gunpowder and other supplies for the *Enrica.* Dudley telegraphed this information to Adams and also personally informed the collector of customs' office of the tug's activities. The consul then wrote Price Edwards a formal request to seize both the tug and the *Enrica.* Edwards, as Dudley expected, declined to act without direction from the Board of Customs. Dudley then sent a message to U.S. consuls and ministers in Atlantic coast nations announcing the "Confederate Privateer's" departure on a "piratical cruise." Describing the vessel as a screw steamer, bark-rigged, built of oak, about two hundred feet long, having a shield figurehead with a cross on a red background, he cautioned them to be vigilant and prevent her from being fitted out in their jurisdiction. He also asked they report any information about the ship's movement to the federal government.[40]

Rumors quickly circulated of sightings at Queenstown, Holyhead, Point Lynas, and other ports along the British, Irish, and Welsh coasts. Dudley reported to Seward, "Some say she is still in the channel others that she has gone to sea and to meet one of the steamers in mid-ocean and there receive her armament but there [*sic*] are not I think reliable."[41] The consul rushed agents to check out the reports, but to no avail. He believed one sighting from a Holyhead lighthouse was the *Tuscarora,* not the *Enrica.* By August 6, nine days after she had sailed, he had heard of the ship being off the Giants' Causeway and that she would attempt to run into a Southern port, probably Savannah. The *Tuscarora,* too, chased rumors, but Captain T. A. Craven, her skipper, learned on August 8 that the "*290*" had sailed north around Ireland and had eluded him.[42]

Upon returning to Liverpool from northern Ireland, Bulloch contracted for the *Bahama,* which was bringing Captain Semmes from Nassau, to take Semmes and his officers to Terceira. Semmes arrived in Liverpool on August 8. Bulloch decided to accompany him to meet the *Enrica* to ease Semmes's transition to ship's captain. They sailed on August 13 aboard the *Bahama* and reached Praya, on the island of Terceira, on August 20. The *Enrica* and *Agrippina* lay at anchor in the bay awaiting their arrival. With mild days and calm seas, the crew quickly transferred the armament to the *Enrica,* finishing by 10 o'clock on Friday, August 22. Bulloch then sent the *Agrippina* back to England for coal to resupply the cruiser, but several of her crewmen stayed behind to help the other crew members transfer coal from the *Bahama* to the *Enrica.*[43]

Two days later, on Sunday, August 24, the two ships sailed slowly out into international waters beyond the three-mile territorial limit. Semmes invited all the crewmen aboard the *Enrica*. She had been scrubbed and shined until she sparkled in the August sun. All the officers wore their new Confederate uniforms. Semmes mounted a gun carriage and read his commission as a Confederate Navy captain and then his orders to take command of the newly christened C.S.S. *Alabama*. He finished his speech, the gunner fired a salute, the Confederate Stars and Bars replaced the British flag atop the mast, the band played "Dixie," and the crew gave three cheers. After this inspiring display, Semmes released the crew from their contracts and offered them free passage to Liverpool if they so chose. He then talked of the Confederates' cause, their attempt to dissolve a legal contract peacefully had been prevented by force and their homeland invaded. The *Alabama*, he explained, would prey on Northern commerce, not as a privateer but as a Confederate warship with strict discipline aboard. But there would also be good food, grog twice a day, and pay, in gold, at twice the Royal Navy wages, which were about 1 1/2 British pounds sterling per week. Finally, Semmes concluded, "We are going to burn, sink and destroy the commerce of the United States. Your prize-money will be divided proportionately, according to each man's rank, something similar to the English Navy. There is Mr. Kell [Semmes's executive officer] on deck, and all who are desirous of going with me, let them go aft, and give Mr. Kell their names." By midnight about eighty crewmen had signed on, a small crew but adequate to begin the *Alabama*'s journey. Semmes would fill out his crew by recruiting sailors from the ships he captured. Bulloch then bid Captain Semmes "a cordial adieu, with heartfelt prayers for his success" and boarded the *Bahama* for the return trip to Liverpool. Semmes set course to the northeast.[44]

Semmes immediately began drilling his diverse gang of civilian sailors into a proper naval crew. On September 5, less than two weeks after leaving Terceira, the *Alabama* spotted the *Ocmulgee*, a New England whaler laying alongside her kill. Semmes ordered his second lieutenant, Richard Armstrong, to board the whaler and return with its captain and the ship's papers. Semmes confirmed the ship's Yankee ownership, ordered her crew aboard the *Alabama*, removed the food and other stores he could use, and burned her the following morning. He then paroled the *Ocmulgee*'s officers and crew after they promised not to fight against the Confederacy, stocked their whaleboats with food and water, and released them within a few miles of Flores, the westernmost of the Azores islands.

This scene would be repeated many times during the next eighteen months, only the victims' names changed. Between September 7, 1862, and April 27, 1864, the *Alabama* built a reputation as the world's most feared commerce raider. She was to travel over seventy-five thousand miles, never visit a Confederate port, and capture sixty-four Union ships with an estimated value of $5,163,143. One of these ships Semmes sold, another he commissioned, ten he released on bond to be paid at war's end, and the other fifty-two he burned at sea. He normally bonded a ship when he had more prisoners than his ship could safely hold. The *Alabama* also sank the U.S.S. *Hatteras* in a one-sided battle near Galveston Bay.

Far greater loss to the American maritime industry came from over three hundred other ships' changing their registry to British to avoid capture. Only Northern ships were subject to capture by the commerce raiders. Many shipowners either sold their vessels to British merchants or reregistered them in Great Britain. Semmes often reviewed such transactions and then decided if the change in ownership was legitimate or simply a ruse to avoid capture. If he determined it was a ruse, he destroyed the ship anyway. It is interesting that the British never protested Semmes's acting as his own court the way they had with Lieutenant Fairfax during the *Trent* Affair. U.S. shipping would not recover until well into the twentieth century. But despite the *Alabama*'s success, U.S. Navy Secretary Welles refused to weaken the blockade to pursue her.[45]

After nearly two years at sea, the *Alabama* needed extensive repairs, so Semmes brought her into Cherbourg, France. The U.S.S. *Kearsarge* quickly learned of the infamous raider's whereabouts and moved to block her escape. After careful consideration, Semmes decided to confront the *Kearsarge* rather than allow his illustrious beloved ship to be blockaded in the harbor. On 10 o'clock Sunday morning, June 19, 1864, the *Alabama* sailed out into international waters to meet the *Kearsarge*. The battle, which began about 11 o'clock, lasted just over an hour. Although the *Alabama* fired more often, two years at sea had dampened her powder and made her shots less effective. Shortly after noon, a white flag appeared on the *Alabama*'s boom and the *Kearsarge* ceased firing. Semmes and most of his crew survived, he even managed to elude capture when the *Deerhound,* a privately owned English ship, plucked him out of the water and carried him to England. The *Alabama,* however, sank at 12:24.[46]

Although the *Alabama*'s career ended at Cherbourg, Dudley continued gathering information on her nature and her origin, as he had since the ship's escape from Liverpool. After the *Alabama* eluded Captain Craven aboard the U.S.S. *Tuscarora* and while the other Union vessels searched for her, the lawyer in Dudley systematically built a case against her with the belief that eventually there would come a "day of reckoning." When the *Bahama* sailed with Bulloch, Semmes, and his officers, Dudley recorded the fact and furnished a description for the Union Navy to aid in her capture. He also photographed a painting the Lairds had made of the *Alabama* and forwarded that to the Navy Department. In September 1862 he obtained an affidavit from Henry Redden, a boatswain who sailed to Terceira with the *Alabama* but declined to sign on for her extended cruise. After Semmes discharged Clarence Yonge (the paymaster Bulloch had hired) for drunkenness and misappropriating ship's funds, Dudley financially supported Yonge for several months in exchange for his affidavit and agreement to testify against the ship. Yonge eventually returned to the United States and worked in the Treasury Department in Washington. In January 1864, the consul obtained an affidavit from John Latham, an *Alabama* crew member, and published it as "A Statement of one of the Crew of the Alabama, now residing in Liverpool." He did not stop gathering evidence against the *Alabama* even after the *Kearsarge* sank her. He sought a prior connection between the *Alabama* and the *Deerhound* to prove the English plotted with Semmes to evade capture. Although never able to substantiate this connection, Dudley's other evidence would be critical if ever there was a "Day of Reckoning."[47]

THE *ALEXANDRA*

*Test Case for
the British Foreign
Enlistment Act*

4

Dudley learned of the *Alexandra* in mid-October 1862. Although he at first believed she would be ready in January, subsequent information convinced him it would be February at the earliest, but he entertained little hope of stopping her. He had expended great effort and built the strongest case he could against the *Alabama,* but British authorities maintained he had to obtain legal proof of the ship's ownership and of her warlike nature and intentions before they would act against her. They had never tested their Foreign Enlistment Act in court and were reluctant to interfere with Liverpool's important shipbuilding industry. When they finally did move, it was too late. Dudley had also discovered two ironclads in the Laird shipyard the previous July, but their progress was even slower. So, after the escape of the *Alabama,* there was little suspicious shipbuilding that required Dudley's immediate attention.[1]

On the diplomatic front, however, a crisis was unfolding. Even as Foreign Secretary Russell weighed Dudley's evidence against the *Alabama,* Parliament debated Southern recognition. On July

18, William Lindsay, a pro-Confederacy member of Parliament, proposed that Great Britain offer to mediate the American dispute, asserting that permanent separation between the two factions would eventually benefit the slaves. Northern supporters countered that English workers perceived intervention would "produce a stain on the antislavery flag of England." While Parliament debated, the British cabinet discussed the country's future role in ending the conflict. By July 1862 nearly everyone in England, even antislavery advocates, believed the North could not subdue the rebelling states and Great Britain would soon lead European recognition of the Confederacy.[2]

Prime Minister Palmerston, Foreign Secretary Russell, and Chancellor of the Exchequer William Gladstone, the cabinet's leading members, all considered the Northern cause hopeless. Even though Russell and Gladstone personally hated slavery, they equally abhorred the carnage of America's Civil War battles. They believed that, by interceding, England could stop the war and then bring greater pressure on the newly independent South to free the slaves or at least improve their living and working conditions. As Parliament adjourned in early August, Palmerston and Russell formulated an armistice proposal. Russell suggested October as the proper time, the foreign secretary would be on the Continent until then, accompanying the grieving Queen Victoria whose husband Prince Albert had just died.[3]

The Union defeat at the Second Battle of Bull Run in late August reinforced Palmerston's resolve to recommend an "arrangement upon the basis of separation" to the dis-United States. Russell suggested mediation "with a view of the recognition of the independence of the Confederates." Palmerston decided they should await word on the outcome of General Robert E. Lee's Army of Northern Virginia advance into Maryland. Lee threatened Washington, and if the Northern capital fell there could be no question that it was time to intercede. The prime minister scheduled a cabinet meeting for October 23 or 30 to receive intervention proposals.[4]

Although not privy to these discussions, the Northerners in England knew from the parliamentary debates and conversations on the street that a British arbitration or armistice proposal was possible, even likely. After the second loss at Bull Run,

Dudley wrote Seward that Liverpool considered a "southern Confederacy" as "a fixed fact. . . . The question of recognition and cessation of hostilities only regarded as a matter of time." Secretary of State Seward prepared Minister Adams for such an eventuality: "If Britain, alone or jointly with other powers, approach with any proposal to dictate, or to mediate, or to advise, or even to solicit or persuade, you will answer that you are forbidden to debate, to hear, or in any way receive, entertain or transmit, any communication of the kind."[5]

After General George McClellan's Army of the Potomac repelled Lee's army at Sharpsburg, Maryland, on September 17, 1862, in the Battle of Antietam, Palmerston became "lukewarm" to intervening. He wrote Russell that the Confederate advance had been checked, and since the "real course of recent events" was unclear he proposed waiting "ten days or a fortnight" to learn more before acting. The prime minister later suggested delaying until the spring when military actions against the United States, which would likely result from British recognition of the South, would be easier.[6]

Russell and Gladstone, however, wanted to press ahead with a mediation proposal. Gladstone, in what proved to be a breach in protocol and not a statement of official policy, declared at Newcastle on October 8, "Jefferson Davis and other leaders of the South have made an army; they are making, it appears, a navy; and they have made what is more than either, they have made a nation." Gladstone's remarks prompted Dudley to comment,"[F]our vessels building for the Rebel Navy at this port . . . with the one at Glasgow, certainly warranted Mr. Gladstone in saying . . . 'that the south were constructing a Navy.' If he had have said England was constructing one for the south it would have been nearer the truth." Other cabinet members quickly made it clear that Gladstone did not speak for them. Palmerston consulted the Earl of Derby and Benjamin Disraeli, leaders of the political opposition, and learned they would not support mediation. The prime minister then reverted to his original stance that the South must win its independence on the battlefield. When Minister Adams approached Lord Russell on October 23 asking if Britain was preparing to recognize the Confederacy,

Russell replied that, for the present, the government would maintain its neutrality and make no offer of mediation. But he would not commit his government to any long-term course of action.[7]

Dudley, meanwhile, continued investigating the gunboat in the William Miller and Sons boatyard. Since Miller and Sons had built the *Oreto,* another wooden gunboat under construction there immediately aroused Dudley's suspicions. He described her as about 240 feet long, light draft, and constructed to "run very fast." In a letter to Secretary Seward, Dudley noted that the construction was supervised by Captain Alexander Duguid, who had sailed the *Oreto* to Nassau to meet its captain, John Maffitt. Construction had just begun when Dudley discovered the gunboat, but a double crew was working to complete her as soon as possible.[8]

Determined to act more quickly this time, Dudley again retained Squarey to prepare the case against the vessel and alerted Minister Adams and Foreign Secretary Russell on November 20 of her existence and his suspicions. He reported to Seward that Fraser, Trenholm and Company, whose financial dealings for the South were well known, had signed the contract and were paying for construction. Fawcett, Preston and Company, builders of the *Alabama*'s engines, were making engines and furnishing the armament for this new ship. Dudley had no doubts she was destined for "the Rebels" as "an armed privateer or pirate to cruise against the United States and to destroy our commerce." He doubted the British would act to stop her. On March 20, 1863, he wrote Seward, "I have no idea that we shall succeed in stopping her, do not think the government are disposed to aid us in the least or that they will interfere if we should obtain evidence. But it seems to me that we should leave nothing undone on our part, that we should do our duty whether they do or not."[9]

In late December Dudley personally visited the Miller shipyard. He learned the ship would launch in February 1863 and that Fawcett, Preston and Company, not Fraser, Trenholm and Company had contracted for the vessel. But Fraser, Trenholm and Company supplied the money. She was very similar to the *Oreto,* with a thick wooden hull and built for speed as well as strength. His inspection confirmed to his satisfaction that she was intended to be a Confederate warship.[10]

Dudley managed to obtain approximate dimensions and a good description of the vessel in February 1863. At 145 feet long and 26 feet wide, she was a good deal smaller than his earlier estimate and not as large as either the *Florida* or the *Alabama*. But her two 90-horsepower engines would drive her along at fifteen to sixteen knots, which was faster than either of the bigger vessels. Constructed of oak and teak, she had iron deck beams over her engine and boilers. She was rigged as a topsail schooner and, like the two previous raiders, had a retractable propeller. Dudley enclosed a draftsman's drawing of the ship in his letter to Seward. He had heard she might escape by sailing before completed, but he promised to do everything possible to stop her.[11]

Miller and Sons launched the gunboat on March 7, 1863. Fawcett, Preston and Company immediately began installing the engines. After his failure to stop the *Alabama,* Dudley doubted his chances with this new vessel. Even Squarey did not believe they could succeed if the English government held fast and required the United States to gather the damning evidence against her. Dudley expressed his disillusionment to Seward, telling him "the government gives us no aid and leaves us to make out the case in the best way we can, and having no process to compel persons to testify we cannot obtain one particle of evidence except such as is voluntarily given and the government requires us to produce legal evidence before they will move."[12]

Dudley received another disappointment when he consulted R. P. Collier, who had given him such encouragement and excellent advice previously. The consul traveled to Exeter, in the south of England, to meet with the barrister. Collier informed Dudley that the government censured him for expressing an opinion on the *Alabama*. Also, Collier had recently received an appointment as admiralty counsel and he might have to advise the government on this new vessel. So after hearing Dudley's evidence, Collier reluctantly declined to assist him, fearing a conflict of interest. Instead, he recommended Robert Lush, whom Dudley recognized as one of the "most eminent lawyers in the Kingdom."[13]

Dudley immediately took the train to London, where he met with Minister Adams before seeing Lush. Adams, too, felt disillusioned by the British government's attitude on shipbuilding for the Confederacy and doubted the efficacy of Dudley's further efforts. The minister, however, agreed with Dudley's consulting Lush. In England one could not approach a barrister except through an attorney. Dudley, therefore, hired an attorney who helped him consult with Lush, who then reviewed the information on the nature of the ship, which Dudley now believed to be called the *Alexandria,* and the circumstantial evidence linking her to the Confederacy. He expressed the opinion that only by questioning the builders under oath could Dudley obtain sufficient legal evidence to justify stopping the ship, but English law provided no procedure by which the United States could force the builders to testify. All Lush could advise was for Dudley to gather statements from people "who speaking from their own knowledge" could prove that the ship was "being built for warlike purposes under" Bulloch's direction and connect him to the *Florida* and the *Alabama.*[14]

Despite this discouraging news, Dudley doggedly pressed ahead compiling whatever information he could. He considered it a great hardship and injustice that the British government would not act until the United States furnished legal evidence but provided no means for the United States to obtain it. But, he explained to Secretary Seward, "If we should succeed in obtaining evidence and then they refuse to interfere it will place them in the wrong." Again, he seemed to be building a case for "the day of reckoning" that he expected would eventually come. He promised to do his best and hoped the State Department would approve his actions.[15]

On March 28, 1863, Dudley presented his witnesses to Liverpool Collector of Customs Price Edwards and formally asked him to "seize and arrest" the *Alexandra.* Dudley himself affirmed that William C. Miller and Sons, the same people who had built the *Florida* for the "so-called Confederate States," were now constructing a similar one. Since the company building the engines furnished those of the *Florida,* the firm supplying the money also did so for the *Florida,* and James Bulloch, a well-known Confederate agent, was apparently superintending the construction of the *Alexandra,* Dudley believed this proved the ship was intended as a Confederate gunboat to "cruise and commit hostilities against" the United States and its citizens.[16]

The affidavits submitted with the application included that of John De Costa, a shipping agent who swore he had personal contact with Miller and Sons, who told him the *Alexandra* would be fitted out as a gunboat for the Confederacy to capture and destroy U.S. shipping. Oliver R. Mumford, an American master mariner, attested that based on his twenty-eight years' experience the vessel was built and being fitted out for war purposes. Neil Black, an experienced ship's carpenter who also examined the vessel, swore she was a warship and that he had been told she was meant for the Confederate States. Private detective Matthew Maguire claimed various workmen for Miller and Sons had told him this was a gunboat built for Southerners. Finally, Thomas Hutson, a boatman, swore the ship was a gunboat and that a ship's carpenter told him she was for the Confederate States. Dudley now believed he had submitted a stronger case than he had dared hope to and engaged Squarey, Lush, and another prominent barrister, a Mr. Milward, to evaluate his evidence. He forwarded copies of his application and the supporting affidavits to Minister Adams.[17]

In the package to Adams, Dudley included several incriminating letters he had received the preceding day. The wife of Clarence Yonge, the *Alabama*'s paymaster and Bulloch's former assistant, had recently arrived in Liverpool. At her hotel she met George T. Chapman, an alleged Southern-sympathizing Northerner, and gave him some of her husband's papers including Yonge's commission, his assignment aboard the *Alabama*, and a letter from Bulloch to Confederate Navy Secretary Mallory. Chapman, who would eventually become Dudley's paid agent, recognized the documents' possible legal value and immediately brought them to the consul. Adams passed the papers and affidavits on to Foreign Secretary Russell on March 30.[18]

When Dudley consulted with Lush, his barrister in London, concerning the strength of his case against the *Alexandra,* Lush considered the sworn affidavits damning enough to "warrant the seizure of the vessel." He cautioned Dudley, however, that many of the statements were based on hearsay and the courts would not accept them as legal evidence. When Dudley visited the legation the next day, he found Clarence Yonge himself talking with legation assistant secretary Benjamin Moran asking to swear allegiance to the United States. He apparently had left the *Alabama* and wanted to return to America. He seemed willing to discuss his recent activity aboard the *Alabama,* and Dudley and Minister Adams quickly concluded Yonge's testimony would be of great value. Without revealing he had the papers from Yonge's wife, Dudley took the former paymaster to the consul's hotel room where an attorney took his affidavit. Yonge detailed his cruise aboard the *Alabama* and described Confederate ship purchasing and building activities in England, especially Bulloch's role in the *Alabama*'s construction and fitting out. Dudley concluded he now had enough evidence to convict the Lairds, Bulloch, the companies Fraser, Trenholm and Company and Fawcett, Preston and Company, and others of violating the Foreign Enlistment Act, "if there was any disposition on the part of this government to take it up, and punish those who violate their laws." At Adams's direction, Dudley paid Yonge's food and lodging costs and planned to book his passage to the United States the following week.[19]

Three days later, on April 6, 1863, Adams wired Dudley simply, "The Alexandra is stopped I will write in full in todays mail." The following morning, the *Liverpool Journal of Commerce* described how a customs surveyor, E. Morgan, boarded the ship, painted a broad arrow on her mast, and assumed possession. Dudley wrote Secretary Seward the good news on April 8, detailing the events. It was the Home Office (not the Lords of the Treasury, who controlled the customs system) who directed Liverpool's mayor to detain the ship and gather evidence against her. Russell apparently wanted to ensure quicker and more positive action than previously against the *Alabama*. Dudley did not know whether the United States or Great Britain would prosecute the case, but at Adams's direction he would assist the local police officer handling the proceedings. Squarey, whom Dudley consulted, agreed he should aid the investigation in every way possible and advised keeping Yonge available in England until after the trial. Dudley considered Yonge "a reckless and uncertain kind of man—quite likely a bad man," but he agreed to £6 sterling per week compensation until the trial and then to pay for his and his wife's passage to the United States. It seemed prudent to move him to a small town "in the interior" to "get him out of the way of the other side." Dudley must have been especially pleased when Assistant Secretary Frederick Seward, writing for his father, congratulated him and noted President Lincoln's "high appreciation" of the consul's accomplishing "this important object."[20]

The decision to stop the *Alexandra* probably surprised Dudley, Adams, and many others. The Foreign Enlistment Act had not changed, and there had still been no court test case redefining it. Although Russell was foreign secretary, he and Palmerston conferred and the prime minister had the final approval on important foreign policy decisions. Apparently the two concluded it was time for the Crown's best legal minds to determine what the act permitted and prohibited. Palmerston had previously served fifteen years as a pragmatic foreign secretary, who weighed policy based on England's best interests. England, as the world's greatest maritime power, had long supported the rights of belligerents. Palmerston knew that defending a neutral nation's right to build commerce raiders to prey on a belligerent nation's shipping offered short-term benefits by possibly preventing Great Britain from having to pay for damages caused by the *Alabama* and her sister ships. But, as the world's largest maritime nation, England had much to lose in the future if the situation were reversed. By April 4, 1863, the *Alabama* had already burned forty-one ships valued at about $2 million.[21] In the future, several such ships—built in neutral American shipyards for France, Prussia, or some other nation with which England was at war—could do considerably more damage to the larger British maritime fleet. Perhaps Dudley's evidence, Adams's persistence, and Seward's belligerence prompted the two British leaders to reconsider their country's position. Palmerston, always seeking to do what was best for England, had several practical reasons for changing his policy. By accepting the Union's argument, Great Britain, who often found herself at war, could set a precedent further limiting neutral rights during wartime and she could accomplish this long-held goal with the support of the United States, the traditional defender of neutral nations' rights.[22]

Also, the United States had recently revived a bill authorizing the president to commission privateers to attack merchant ships. Congress considered such action in July 1862 shortly before the *Alabama*'s escape and enacted it in March 1863. Since the Confederate states had no merchant ships, neutral shipping would be the likely targets if the blockade were broken. Palmerston and Russell realized the impact a fleet of privateers could have on the huge British maritime industry, the privateers' most likely target.

Palmerston's move could ease tensions with the United States and allow England greater freedom of action in Europe. Increasing friction between Denmark and Prussia over Schleswig-Holstein, duchies united in 1848 but with separate histories and allegiances, threatened to develop into war. Prussian leader Otto von Bismarck envisioned himself as the chancellor of a unified German republic with Schleswig-Holstein as part of it. Denmark and Prussia had fought in 1848, before England's intercession led to a temporary truce. The war resumed in 1849 but stopped the following year without deciding the duchies' fate. The 1855 Treaty of London, signed by the major European powers (but not the German Confederation), assigned the duchies to Denmark's King Frederick VII. Pressured by Schleswig's Danes, Frederick proclaimed Denmark's constitution valid for both duchies. The German Confederation protested and Frederick recanted his proclamation, but neither side considered the matter settled. Indeed another Danish-Prussian war began in January 1864.

Another factor possibly influenced the prime minister and foreign secretary to a lesser degree. The Antietam battle outcome that delayed Palmerston's decision to intercede in the American conflict also signaled Abraham Lincoln to issue his Emancipation Proclamation. On September 22, 1862, Lincoln declared that all slaves in states still in rebellion against the Union on January 1, 1863, would be free as of that date. Southern supporters in England argued Lincoln's declaration would emancipate no slaves but, instead, would incite slave uprisings and the slaughter of white women and children. British antislavery organizations and Union supporters celebrated the proclamation as proving the North fought the noble fight against slavery. Although Dudley noted the proclamation "produced a profound sensation . . . throughout the Kingdom" and settled the question of English intervention, there is little evidence it directly influenced Palmerston's decision to stop the *Alexandra*. The Emancipation Proclamation may have found favor with many British workers, and the prime minister, as head of a coalition government, was sensitive to voters' opinions. Still, public opinion would not sway him from doing what he considered best for England. Besides, the working class had no vote and very little political clout. Several factors, therefore, probably influenced the decision to stop the *Alexandra*.[23]

Dudley learned within a few days that England would prosecute the case, but he doubted the sincerity of those in charge. Customs solicitor F. J. Hammel, the same individual who had repeatedly rejected evidence against the *Alabama*, would prosecute the Crown's case. After spending two days with Hammel examining evidence, Dudley concluded that the solicitor "had no heart in the matter." Furthermore, the detective-in-charge, E. Morgan, worked for the chief surveyor of customs, who was none other than William Miller himself. Dudley noted that Morgan had "as yet done nothing." The consul believed "they design to fizzle the case out and do nothing."[24]

Still determined to build the strongest case possible against the *Alexandra*, Dudley employed William Downward, a London detective, to seek more evidence. He engaged Squarey to assist Hammel in the prosecution and hired Lush to prepare a separate legal brief for the court. Additionally, William Evarts, an American lawyer the State Department had sent to England as a goodwill ambassador and Minister Adams's legal advisor, completed the American trial team.[25]

In response to a request from Hammel, Dudley asked the State Department for incriminating letters the Union had intercepted from Confederate Treasury Secretary Christopher Memminger and Navy Secretary Mallory discussing Confederate shipbuilding and Bulloch's role in it, as well as for someone to verify their signatures. Hammel also wanted a ship's captain from a vessel captured by the *Florida* and another from an *Alabama* victim. Dudley urged Secretary Seward to comply with Hammel's request, fearing that a failure to do so would "be used as a pretext by the British government to justify them not prosecuting."

Concluding that the British government had left it to him to gather the evidence, Dudley and his detectives gradually found more people willing to testify as to the *Alexandra*'s warlike nature and her Confederate ownership. As in the earlier cases his witnesses had little direct knowledge, and hearsay did not count as legal proof. He felt the Crown might call the ship's builders and outfitters to testify, but if they failed to tell the truth there would be no conviction. Dudley realized he had developed a stronger case against both the *Oreto* and the *Alabama* than he could ever build against the *Alexandra* since workmen at Miller and Sons were unwilling to speak against their employer. One point was in his favor, however. The Court of the Exchequer in London and a Westminster jury would hear the case, not a jury from Liverpool, where nearly everyone seemed to favor the South.[26]

At this point, the prosecution's case suffered a seemingly devastating blow. Liverpool's head constable turned over Dudley's evidence to the city's mayor, who shared it with two members of the Watch Committee, the citizens group that oversaw the city police force. These members also belonged to Liverpool's pro-Confederacy Southern Club and were close friends of Charles Prioleau, the partner in Fraser, Trenholm and Company and an associate of James Bulloch. No doubt the defendants now knew everything the prosecution intended to use against them, something English law did not require the prosecution to disclose. Squarey asked Liverpool's town clerk to confirm or deny this had happened, and the clerk refused to respond. Everyone soon knew the answer anyway as someone brought the information before the town council and local newspapers printed it. Dudley could hardly believe officials would so violate the public's trust to "utterly defeat the ends of justice." Still he vowed to continue collecting information, but from now on, he would withhold it from local officials.[27]

Bulloch, meanwhile, was also busy. He knew Dudley was building his case on the false premise that Bulloch had contracted for and had supervised the building of the *Alexandra*, when in fact he had not. Charles Prioleau and his partners in Fraser, Trenholm and Company decided they would have Miller and Sons build a commerce raider as a gift for the Confederacy. Prioleau asked Lieutenant John Hamilton (who remained in Liverpool after his commission aboard the *Alabama* was voided when Semmes replaced Bulloch as captain) to supervise the *Alexandra*'s construction, and Hamilton agreed. Fraser, Trenholm and Company then contracted with Fawcett, Preston and Company, the engineering firm that made the engines for the *Oreto* and the *Alabama,* and that company then hired William Miller and Sons to construct the ship itself. The defendants in the *Alexandra* case, therefore, were Fawcett, Preston and Company, the contractors. Knowing that defending the case would cost far more than any fine the court would levy against the contractors, Bulloch feared Fawcett, Preston and Company would choose not to present a strong defense. Not wanting the English courts to interpret the Foreign Enlistment Act as forbidding belligerent shipbuilding, Bulloch promised to pay part or all of the cost if the company hired the best solicitor available and presented a strong defense. Fawcett, Preston and Company agreed and engaged Sir Hugh Cairnes, whom many considered the best lawyer in Great Britain. Having previously served as solicitor general, he would later become attorney general, lord chancellor, and the Conservative party leader. John Karslake, another eminent barrister known for his ability to cross-examine opposing witnesses, and the queen's counsel, George Mellish, completed the defense attorneys.[28]

As the date approached for the trial, Dudley was "much astonished" by a June 4 letter from Hammel to Squarey. The customs' solicitor related that the Crown's prosecutors—himself, the attorney general, the solicitor general, and the queen's advocate—had met the previous day expecting to review all the evidence and examine the prosecution witnesses. Since neither the evidence nor the witnesses were present, the prosecution concluded Dudley and the U.S. legal team lacked confidence in the Crown's officers. They threatened to "wash their hands of the case altogether" if Squarey did not send Yonge and other important witnesses and documents to London "forthwith." The letter surprised Dudley, since he had not been informed the meeting was to take place. He claimed he had cooperated in every way and had held back nothing, even though he had vowed earlier to do so. He told Minister Adams, in fact, he had offered the Crown copies of the documents only to be told they already had them. Not wanting to give the Crown any excuse to withdraw from the case, Dudley ordered Squarey to immediately forward the items in question and the consul himself brought Yonge to meet with the Crown's law officers the next day. This seemed to ease tensions between the two legal teams as they prepared for the trial.[29]

Dudley, "doing all within [his] power to obtain a conviction," found two people who could verify Memminger's signature and captains of ships captured by the *Florida* and the *Alabama*. The intercepted correspondence that connected Bulloch and the Confederacy with Liverpool shipbuilding had not arrived from the State Department, but Dudley had newspaper copies of the letters. Still, the consul expressed doubts about the prosecution's strategy. He believed the Crown should call not only the witnesses he had found, but also Bulloch, Prioleau and other Fraser, Trenholm and Company officers, Fawcett, Preston and Company officials, even William Miller. "We should go into the enemy's camp, and place every one of the parties implicated on the witness stand." If this did not help convict the contractors, at least, it would expose to the world England's role in Confederate shipbuilding. The Crown's prosecutors, however, disagreed, and the consul lamented that he was not in a position to dictate, he could only suggest.[30]

On June 22, 1863, the trial began in Westminster in Chief Baron Sir Jonathan Frederick Pollock's Court of the Exchequer before a special jury. The first witness, a Liverpool customs official, recounted details of the ship's seizure. Five former employees of either William Miller and Sons or Fawcett, Preston and Company described the ship's construction and nature and Confederate Navy Lieutenant Hamilton's role in the process. Royal Navy Captain Edward Inglefield then attested that the ship was unsuitable for commercial sailing but was easily adaptable into a warship. John De Costa, who had earlier sworn affidavits against the *Alabama* and the *Alexandra*, testified that William Miller himself had told him the *Alexandra* was a gunboat for the Confederacy. Another ship's craftsman then confirmed earlier statements that this ship was built like a gunboat.[31]

The prosecution saved its star witnesses until last. George Chapman recounted his visits to Fraser, Trenholm and Company and conversations with Bulloch and Prioleau. Chapman's prior acquaintance with Bulloch and Hamilton from their days in the U.S. Navy gained him some credibility with them and gave him limited access to the Miller and Laird shipyards. He also explained how he had acquired Yonge's letters and described their content tying Bulloch and Fraser, Trenholm and Company to the South and the *Alabama*. Clarence Yonge, the prosecution's last witness, knew little about the *Alexandra,* but he could relate in great detail the roles of Bulloch and of the Fraser, Trenholm and Fawcett, Preston companies in building and fitting out the *Alabama*. Of note, the prosecution did not call Bulloch, Hamilton, Prioleau, or anyone from Fawcett, Preston and Company to testify. All the witnesses, except the customs official and Captain Inglefield, were people Dudley had located and convinced to give testimony.[32]

The defense team's strategy was to call no witnesses, concentrating instead on destroying the prosecution's case during cross-examination. Chapman and Yonge warranted special attention. Cairns portrayed Chapman as a man willing to betray his friends for money. Yonge, according to the defense team, deserted his ship, married a widow, spent her money, then abandoned her, and finally sold his services and his testimony to his country's enemy. In his summation after Yonge's testimony, Cairns attacked the character and veracity of the prosecution's witnesses and asserted that the Crown had not proved the *Alexandra* was intended for the Confederacy. Neither issue really mattered, he said, since the Foreign Enlistment Act did not prohibit a company from "building" a warship.[33]

The judge, Chief Baron Jonathan Pollock, followed a strict interpretation of the law and agreed with Cairns's argument. He instructed the jury that building a ship for a belligerent did not violate the Foreign Enlistment Act, the offender must build and arm a warship in British waters. Citing the case of the *Alabama,* he considered there had been no violation since she sailed from Liverpool unarmed. "If you think the object really was to build a ship in obedience to an order, and in compliance with a contract, leaving it to those who bought it to make what use they thought fit of it, then it appears to me that the foreign enlistment act has not been in any degree broken." Dudley summed up the judge's interpretation as "they can build as many war vessels as they pleased for either of the belligerents provided they did not arm them in England." With Chief Baron Pollock's jury instructions, the verdict for the defendants was anticlimactic.[34]

Dudley acknowledged the Crown's attorneys "displayed a certain degree of earnestness," but he considered the prosecution to be "exceedingly weak." Lush, although present throughout the trial, took no part in the proceedings. Hammel and the Crown's law officers insisted on conducting the case themselves, without help. Dudley noted that the prosecution did not call many witnesses who were available in court and failed to adequately question others. He explained to Seward, "Points being directly upon the issue were never opened and not more than one half the testimony in the case was introduced." When he asked the prosecutors why they pursued this strategy, they responded that they considered their case already proved. Dudley complained, "I have never seen any suit of one half the importance or magnitude of this so poorly put to the court and jury." Then he acknowledged that even if all the evidence had been presented, the judge's "extraordinary charge" to the jury ensured the verdict would have been the same.[35]

Contrary to Dudley's expectations, however, Palmerston and Russell did not accept the jury's decision as final. The Crown appealed the verdict to the full Court of the Exchequer and retained the *Alexandra* in custody. At the appeal hearing, the attorneys again argued their case, but without witnesses present. The hearing lasted three weeks, from November 3 to November 23. The four presiding judges were equally divided in their opinions. As was the English custom in case of a tie, the junior jurist withdrew his judgment. The three-judge panel then issued its ruling on January 11, 1864, and again found for the defendants. The Crown appealed this ruling, also. The Court of Exchequer Chamber dismissed the case on a legal technicality and the matter finally reached the ultimate legal authority, the House of Lords, who upheld the decision on April 6, 1864.[36]

After the House of Lords decision, Dudley concluded they agreed that Chief Baron Pollock's interpretation of the Foreign Enlistment Act was the correct one. This meant, according to Dudley, that anyone could legally build a warship for a belligerent, make the guns and other armament, and put them on a tug, the same tug could tow the ship into the English Channel three miles from land, transfer the armament to the ship, and she could sail away to destroy another nation's commercial shipping. He did not believe any "high toned and correct thinking" Englishman could look at this case and be proud of his judicial system.[37]

British authorities released the *Alexandra* on April 25 and paid Fawcett, Preston and Company £3,700 sterling for damages. Dudley kept a close watch on the *Alexandra* as work resumed even before customs returned control on April 27. He noted that she was almost ready to sail and assumed that Lieutenant Hamilton, who was still in Liverpool, would command the ship on her mission as a commerce raider. Even as she gradually added cabins on deck and made other alterations, taking on the appearance and characteristics of a blockade runner, Dudley considered her a pirate preparing to prey on Northern shipping. The news from London consul Freeman Morse that the guns originally built for the *Alexandra* and stored in a London warehouse during her trial had moved to Liverpool seemed to confirm Dudley's suspicions. He surmised she would sail to Nassau or Bermuda looking like a blockade runner, then quickly convert into a commerce raider, and begin sinking Union ships. "They can clear her decks in a day and very soon prepare her for a privateer."[38] He sent Seward photographs and a detailed description of the ship now named *Mary* to aid the American Navy in her capture.

Feeling he had exhausted all avenues to stop the *Alexandra* and with little other Confederate shipbuilding in Liverpool, Dudley sailed on July 16 for the United States and a short vacation to treat his ailing digestive system and tend to personal business affairs. Ironically, the *Scotia* with Dudley aboard passed the *Mary* at sea bound for Nassau. He immediately notified Seward, reminding him the guns originally intended for the *Alexandra* had shipped for Nassau earlier. The ever-diligent consul urged Seward to forward the ship's description and photograph to the navy.[39]

Despite Dudley's convictions to the contrary, Charles Prioleau had abandoned his original purpose of building a commerce raider and giving her to the South. The *Mary* was indeed what she appeared to be: a vessel on a commercial voyage to Bermuda. From there she sailed to Halifax and then returned to Bermuda. On her second visit, the British government showed it still did not accept Chief Baron Pollock's interpretation as final. The local governor ordered the *Mary* seized on December 13, 1864. The court did not release her until after the war had ended. She later became the center of long legal proceedings when Dudley tried to recover the ship, claiming she had been Confederate property.[40]

The *Alexandra* never became a commerce raider and never achieved the notoriety of the *Florida* or the *Alabama*. The *Alexandra* herself was of little importance and would have done minimal damage even if she had escaped. Instead, she gained fame as the test case for the British Foreign Enlistment Act. For Palmerston and Russell, perhaps, it was time they learned if the courts would stop shipyards from building warships for the Confederacy. But their persistence in this case even after the courts decided against them indicates a larger purpose. Among officials of both the North and the South, only James Bulloch seems to have realized the implications of the subtle shift in British policy toward Confederate shipbuilding. Palmerston and Russell were well aware of the two suspicious vessels then building in the Laird shipyard, ironclad ships so formidable they could destroy the Union's blockading squadron. Their escape would almost certainly lead to war between Britain and the United States. If Dudley and Adams were going to stop the two ironclads from sailing, they would have to find some way other than the Foreign Enlistment Act.

THE UNSTOPPABLE IRONCLADS

5

Thomas Dudley learned of the Laird ironclad rams on July 14, 1862, less than a month after Bulloch contracted for them. The consul warned Minister Adams, "Cap. Bulloch has given orders for the construction of two large steam rams to be made shot proof and of sufficient strength to destroy any vessel we have afloat." A few days later he reported their existence to Secretary Seward, adding that the ships were to be "iron or iron clad" and "in the nature of rams." Although Bulloch signed the contract for the two warships in June 1962, the Confederate ironclad program had begun more than a year earlier. Confederate Navy Secretary Mallory envisioned a two-part plan for breaking the Northern blockade of the vital Southern ports. First, commerce raiders attacking Northern merchant ships would weaken the blockade by drawing off naval vessels to pursue the raiders. Second, ironclad ships incorporating the latest technology would destroy the wooden blockaders and perhaps even attack Northern cities.[1]

Mallory knew of the early nineteenth century's five great advances in naval technology. Robert Fulton's experiments with steam power freed ships from reliance on the uncertainties of the wind. The screw propeller, which replaced paddlewheels, allowed ship's designers to place the steam engines below the water line for better protection. Rifled artillery increased naval guns' range and accuracy. Shells that exploded on contact doomed wooden warships to extinction. Iron plating offered protection from exploding shells. These five developments (steam power, the screw propeller, rifled artillery, exploding shells, and iron plating) revolutionized naval warfare in the mid-nineteenth century. Two other significant changes occurred simultaneously. Steam power allowed the reintroduction of the ram, which had been a formidable weapon on oar-driven ships but impractical on wind-dependent ones, and then, the creation of the gun turret made ironclad ships seem even more deadly.

The French proved ironclads' value in the Crimean War against Russia. They had earlier built the first warship powered primarily by steam, with sails for auxiliary power and with a screw propeller. Emperor Napoléon III's chief naval designer, Dupuy de Lome, created the first steam-powered, screw-propeller, armored warship, *La Gloire,* launched in 1859. By 1860 France had begun building six seagoing and nine coastal-defense ironclads. Although France and England were on friendly terms, England realized that *La Gloire* and her sister ships threatened the security of an island nation dependent on wooden ships for protection. The English quickly began constructing their own fleet of ironclads, including the *Warrior,* the *Black Prince,* and eleven other iron-plated oceangoing warships.

Mallory was following this "naval revolution" even before the South seceded. When he became Confederate navy secretary, he knew the South could never build as many ships as the North, but he could rely on new technology to overcome the difference in numbers. On May 9, 1861, he sent Bulloch to Liverpool to buy or build commerce raiders. The secretary ordered Lieutenant James North to England and France a week later to purchase *La Gloire* or a vessel of that class, since the South lacked the expertise to roll the iron plates needed for ironclads. Mallory believed *La Gloire* could single-handedly destroy the

Union's wooden blockading fleet and open Southern ports. He did not realize de Lome had not overcome all the weight distribution and balance problems inherent in ironclad vessels. The builder intended *La Gloire* for operations in European waters only, not for the open seas, for "she rolled a good deal" even in the Mediterranean's relative calm "and shipped considerable water in bad weather."[2]

Secretary Mallory did not take into account the premium both France and England placed on ironclads. Unlike Bulloch, Lieutenant North did not achieve immediate results. He lacked Bulloch's sense of urgency, self-confidence, and ingenuity, but he also faced greater challenges. Mallory had promised North $2 million to purchase ironclads, but the money was not immediately available. Also, given the strategic value both England and France placed on these new weapons, neither country had any available for sale. Instead of seeking alternatives or at least making preliminary arrangements for building the ships when money was available, North seemed content to bide his time and play the role of the tourist while waiting. He and his family spent months sailing aboard the yacht *Camilla,* visiting French museums and galleries, and sightseeing throughout France and England.

In October 1861, during his visit to the South, Bulloch met with Mallory in Richmond. Among other subjects, they discussed ironclad construction in England. Bulloch doubted the British would allow such blatantly obvious warships to be built. These reservations and North's lack of success apparently convinced Mallory to abandon his foreign ironclad-building plan. He acceded to Bulloch's request for command of the first commerce raider and a commission as commander and assigned North to the second raider building in Liverpool. Then came news of the *Trent* and Captain Wilkes's affront to the British flag. For Mallory and many other Southerners, the incident opened the door for British recognition of Confederate independence or at least a more lenient attitude toward Southern shipbuilding in England. The *Trent* Affair renewed Mallory's dreams of an English-built ironclad fleet. In January 1862 he wrote North to continue looking in England for a suitable builder.[3]

The secretary also instructed Bulloch to "direct your attention" to building "iron or steel clad ships in France or England." As he and Bulloch had already discussed, the ships should be of "moderate" size, about two thousand tons displacement, and carry eight to ten guns. Mallory believed the improved relations between England and the Confederacy would now make "construction and delivery of such a vessel" possible. He also asked Bulloch to work with North on this project and promised to "place the funds in England at once," when the plans were in place.[4]

When Bulloch returned to Liverpool, his first priority was getting the *Florida* out of England. But he also investigated the possibility of building ironclads in Liverpool. Fortunately, the Lairds were among the first to build ironclads for the British navy, including one ordered in August 1861. This contract gave the company access to the latest turret and ironclad structural designs and test results for armor-plate resistance to explosive shells. Having already established a friendly personal and business relationship with the Lairds, Bulloch considered them the obvious choice to build the ironclads, if the South decided to construct them in Europe.[5]

Bulloch observed, however, that contrary to Mallory's belief England did not relax the restrictive Foreign Enlistment Act but, instead, enforced it even more rigorously against Confederate operations. He suggested a creative solution to the dilemma in an April 11, 1862, letter to Mallory. The South could build wooden vessels at home, send him scale drawings of the decks and sides, and he would have the iron plates, rivets, bolts, and so on made in England and shipped to the Confederacy for installation. This would cost less, reduce building time, and could never be interpreted as violating the Foreign Enlistment Act. The slow and uncertain communication between Liverpool and Richmond prevented his getting an answer before he received instructions on June 10 to begin constructing two ironclads.[6]

In April 1862, meanwhile, Lieutenant North met George Thomson of the James and George Thomson shipyard on the Clyde River in Glasgow, Scotland. Thomson could build an "armor-clad steamship" to North's specifications. North immediately wrote Mallory asking for the promised $2 million for the contract. Thomson, meanwhile, completed the plans and a model of the proposed ship. The following month Fraser, Trenholm and Company notified North they were sending him approximately $150,000. There were no instructions with the money, so North assumed it was intended for his ironclad. The next day, May 20, he deposited about $100,000 of the cash he received with Thomson. Only later did he learn that Mallory believed North would be captaining the *Alabama* and the $150,000 was his operating fund. This was not the only time that erratic communication hampered Confederate overseas activities. Mallory often had to make decisions on information that was months old, during wartime when situations can change rapidly.

Relations between Bulloch and North were difficult, compounded by personality differences and by North's pettiness upon learning that the newly commissioned Bulloch, who just a few months earlier had been a civilian, now outranked him. This also prevented their working closely together on acquiring ironclads, ships that their country must have to break the blockade and probably in order to survive. North remained committed to building the huge ship he and Mallory had envisioned in May 1861. Bulloch, from conversations with Mallory in October and November 1861, knew that the Confederacy needed smaller vessels to operate in the Southern coastal waters and rivers. Bulloch tried to convince North to build a smaller ship, but North remained adamant, his orders were "specific and preemptory."[7]

He signed the final contract with Thomson on June 1, 1862. The ship, officially known as *Number 61,* was to be 270 feet long with a 20- or 30-foot draft, and would displace 3,200 tons empty and 4,747 tons fully equipped. Like other contemporary steam-powered vessels, North's ship would operate under either steam or wind power. Unfortunately, he overlooked the detail of a retractable screw propeller to make her more efficient under wind power, a flaw that Bulloch could have prevented if they had had a better relationship. *Number 61* would cost £182,000 sterling (about $900,000) to be paid in eight equal installments over the next twelve months, with payments tied to the ship's progress. The Thomsons promised the "Clyde River ram" would be ready for sea by June 1, 1863. Bulloch considered this "Scottish Sea Monster," as she later became known, too big with a draft too deep to serve Confederate needs. He also felt she was too expensive. But North would hear no criticism, especially none from Bulloch.

Bulloch received his orders to build two ironclads just nine days later, on June 10, 1862. Having already consulted with the Lairds and studied the official reports on ironclad experiments, Bulloch knew the size and draft ironclads needed to make them most efficient in coastal waters yet still seaworthy crossing the Atlantic. He determined turret-mounted guns instead of broadside weapons would relieve strain on the ship's sides and place the added weight over the ship's center. His ironclads would be 230 feet long, have a draft of 15 feet fully loaded, displace 1,850 tons, and have 4 1/2-inch iron plating over 12 inches of teak with a 5/8-inch iron inner skin protecting the ships' vital parts. Each ship's two turrets had 5 1/2 inches of armor over 12 inches of teak covering them, and each turret housed two parallel mounted guns capable of firing 220-pound explosive shells. The vessels also sported the feature that gave them their popular names, an iron "ram" approximately seven feet long that rode three or four feet underwater when the ship was in motion. The bowsprit had "a hinge so as to be turned inboard when the ship is to be used as a ram."[8] These ships were unique in that they were the first vessels to incorporate all five of the latest naval advances, in addition to the turrets and the rams. Bulloch later proclaimed, "I confidently believe they would have broken up the blockade completely, and then perhaps they would have paid New York or Boston an unpleasant visit."[9] For ordering two identical ships, the Lairds granted Bulloch a discount of £1,250 sterling, for a total cost of £93,759 each (about $457,500) or about half what North paid for his ship. The first ship was to be ready in March 1863 and the second in May. Bulloch and the Lairds had both consulted their attorneys and received assurance that nothing in these ships' construction constituted "arming" under Chief Baron Pollock's *Alexandra* decision definition. With the preliminary arrangements already in place, Bulloch and the Lairds signed the contract within a few days of Bulloch's receiving Mallory's letter on June 10. The ships would be numbers 294 and 295 built in the Laird shipyard.[10]

Dudley's agents had constantly watched that shipyard as the *Alabama* neared completion and then prepared to sail. So they quickly spotted the *294's* keel laid in the same stocks from which the *Alabama* launched. By July 14 Dudley knew Bulloch had ordered "two large steam rams to be made shot proof and of sufficient strength to destroy any vessel afloat." Although trying to stop the *Alabama* occupied most of his time and energy throughout the summer, he regularly reported on the rams' progress. By August 30 an agent had managed to get into the Laird yard, and Dudley informed Seward that the first ship would be an ironclad, 250 feet long, "and in all particulars finished in the most substantial manner without regard to expense."[11]

A week later he learned of North's ironclad building on the Clyde. A quick visit to Glasgow confirmed his suspicions. He wrote the U.S. ministers throughout Europe—including St. Petersburg and Constantinople, and the consuls general in Alexandria and Athens—asking if the governments to which they were assigned had an ironclad steamer under construction in the Thomson shipyard. By November 4 all except three had replied "no." This information, added to a careless remark made by the *Alabama's* officers to the captain of a ship they destroyed and a Laird workman's comment concerning a Confederate ironclad building on the Clyde, removed all doubt from Dudley's mind.[12]

By December the consul could quite accurately describe *Number 61.* He told Seward her keel was 250 feet long and she displaced over three thousand tons. Her keel and ribs were wrought iron, and her stem post was iron with "an immense ram of solid iron projecting some eight feet just beneath the water line." But Dudley overestimated the cost at £300,000 sterling. He anticipated she would not be ready to sail until June or July 1863. Again he assured Secretary Seward this was a Confederate vessel.[13]

In Liverpool, meanwhile, Dudley kept close watch on the Laird rams. He noted in October the shipyard had employed two full crews, "as many men engaged . . . as can work with advantage," for each ironclad, so there was "no cessation of work neither day or night." He had also discovered that Fawcett, Preston and Company, builders of the *Alabama*'s engines, were also making those for the rams. Dudley grossly underestimated the time needed to construct ironclads, writing that the first should be completed by mid-December. (He later adjusted this to March.) This misinformation is understandable because, as he told Seward, the Lairds were taking "great precaution to keep us ignorant of their doings." They permitted no strangers to visit their yards. He promised to gather evidence against the ships, but the English government's failure to detain the *Alabama* left him with little hope the British would stop the rams.[14]

Matthew Maguire and other operatives had gleaned enough information by December to create a good description of the Laird ironclads. Dudley informed Seward the ships were the same size and dimensions, with a 200-foot keel, 21 1/2-foot depth, and a 37 1/2-foot beam. Like the Clyde River boat, these ships each had a "strong ram of solid wrought iron projecting about 8 feet just under the water line." The engines were 300-horsepower and horizontal. Twelve watertight compartments comprised the hull. The decks and sides were 10-inch teak covered with 1 1/4-inch iron plates and then 4 1/2-inch iron plating over that. The ships bore the numbers 294 and 295. He expected the first to be launched in late February or early March and the second about a month later.[15]

Despite building a case against the *Alexandra* in early 1863, Dudley stayed abreast of the progress of the Laird rams. Again he erred on the side of caution with his estimated launch date. When he updated Seward on March 25, 1863, he anticipated neither would be ready before June. The consul reemphasized the potential danger they represented, stressing that "nothing is being omitted that science or skill can suggest," including two revolving turrets similar to the U.S.S. *Monitor*'s. Dudley wanted to make sure Seward understood that these would be the "most powerful and destructive vessels afloat. . . . You must not deceive yourselves, when finished they will have more power and speed probably than any Iron Clads that have as yet been built, and so protected with steel and armor plates as to be almost invulnerable." The Clyde River ram was "said to be a still more formidable vessel."[16]

Bulloch also closely monitored the rams' construction and regularly reported their development to Richmond. The ever-present possibility that his letters would fall into Northern hands forced him to keep his remarks brief and his statements general. Throughout the last half of 1862 he noted the construction was moving along well, adding in September, "the ships are progressing as rapidly as could be expected, and . . . I am more pleased with them every day." The ships' contract included a provision that allowed Bulloch to modify the plans as new information or advances became known, but even though the ships were of "entirely new design," he only needed to make "immaterial" changes, not "important alterations."[17] In November, stormy weather and foggy days threatened to slow work, but the Lairds built sheds over the rams and installed gas lighting to keep construction on schedule. Bulloch believed the builders were as eager as he was to get them finished when promised.[18]

Even though Bulloch had again contracted with the Lairds as a private individual executing a commercial transaction and he and the builders had consulted legal experts to ensure they were adhering to the Foreign Enlistment Act, he almost immediately realized, "The difficulty of getting them to sea will be very great . . . and I confess that thus far I do not see the means to be adopted."[19] By November he had devised a method that would not violate British law, but he could not explain in a letter lest Dudley learn of his plan and thwart it. He acknowledged the escape would be difficult and differ from that of either the *Florida* or the *Alabama*. Bulloch also advised that the first ship's crew, made up of career officers and a few "non-commissioned officers who are natives of the South, or *bona-fide* citizens of the Confederacy—to give nationality to the crew," should be ready to meet the first ironclad in Madeira in April 1863.[20]

His doubts persisted, however. In January 1863 he feared the British government would "interfere with any attempt to get them out." When, in January 1863, the Foreign Office released the official documents surrounding the *Alabama*'s escape, Bulloch realized only fate, not English law, had prevented her seizure. He wrote Mallory that Lord Russell had said the *Alabama* evaded the law and inferred that England would not allow that to happen again. The foreign minister's orders that customs officials report on all ships building within their district seemed to confirm Bulloch's conclusions. Southern newspaper articles reprinted in the *London Times* reporting that ironclads from England would soon be coming to break the Northern blockade only added to his hopelessness. This feeling carried over into February when he informed his naval secretary, "Think British Government will prevent iron ships leaving, and am much perplexed; object of armoured ships too evident to disguise." But Mallory would soon lift Bulloch's spirits with a seemingly foolproof plan for getting the ironclads away from England and on their way across the Atlantic.[21]

Washington, meanwhile, had begun listening to Dudley's warnings of the destruction the ironclads could wreak if they escaped. In December 1862 John Murray Forbes, a prominent Boston businessman, suggested to the Navy Department that an American merchant travel to England and buy the ironclads, or any other suspicious vessels, under the guise of purchasing them for China, Siam, or some other foreign government. Navy Secretary Gideon Welles supported the idea, but State Secretary Seward, after initially favoring the move, reconsidered and concluded this would make the North guilty of purchasing warships from England and thereby relieve that country of responsibility for the *Alabama*'s damage to Northern shipping. At about the same time, Freeman Morse, the U.S. consul in London, suggested a similar idea with the added ploy of applying greater diplomatic pressure on Great Britain to stop Confederate shipbuilding there. This might alarm the Southern agents into selling their ships then under construction. Morse concluded and everyone agreed that if this worked it would be the easiest and cheapest way to resolve this dangerous question.[22]

Although reluctant to act after hearing Seward's reservations, Welles eventually decided the U.S. Navy had to try and stop the ironclad rams before they reached the American coast. On March 14, 1863. Treasury secretary Salmon Chase telegraphed Forbes to meet him in New York on important business. Chase, Forbes, Welles, and William Aspinwall, a New York merchant and Forbes's friend and associate, met the next morning. The federal government would give the two businessmen $10 million in new government bonds to secure a £1 million loan from Baring Brothers, the Union's European financial agents. Forbes and Aspinwall would use the money to purchase dangerous vessels to keep them from Confederate hands. Their secondary mission was to buy ships the Northern navy might use, if this could be done without compromising Minister Adams's position. Welles instructed the two men not to tell Adams the true nature of their mission so he could continue protesting Confederate activities in England, but they were to work with and confide in Morse and Dudley.[23]

Forbes sailed on March 18, 1863, and reached Liverpool eleven days later. Aspinwall could not sail until the Treasury Department's register signed each of the 12,500 bond certificates. Upon arrival Forbes immediately conferred with Dudley about his activities and any suspicious ships in the area. Forbes concluded the consul needed more money for additional detectives and advanced him £100 sterling, promising more when Aspinwall arrived. He advised Dudley "the pretty liberal use of money" was the most likely way "to be successful." When Aspinwall joined Forbes on April 5, they learned the Confederates had just acquired a $15 million loan through the Emile Erlanger and Company bank in Paris. This at least temporarily relieved any Confederate money problems and any pressure to sell ships under construction. It also ensured that Aspinwall and Forbes could not fulfill their primary mission. If this were not enough, on April 7, only two days after Aspinwall's arrival, the *London Times* wrote of "two well known merchants, one from Boston and one from New York," who had traveled to London, armed with U.S. government bonds to buy "gunboats now building in England for the rebels."[24]

With their primary objective thwarted, Forbes and Aspinwall focused first on improving United States and British relations and maintaining peace between the two nations. Good Anglo-American relations, they insisted to Seward, depended on the North not issuing letters of marque authorizing privateers, a move Congress had authorized and the president just approved. Conversations with British business and political leaders convinced Forbes and Aspinwall that privateers would provoke conflict between the two nations, conflict that could lead to war. The two men also organized and reenergized the U.S. intelligence-gathering activities in England. They divided the country into two zones, with Dudley responsible for the area north of the fifty-third parallel and Morse for the area south. Forbes encouraged Dudley to spend more time gathering information on Confederate shipbuilding and let Wilding attend to day-to-day consulate duties. Forbes assured the consul that Welles would intercede with Seward if the state secretary felt Dudley was neglecting his duties. The two emissaries also developed a code for confidential communication between themselves and Dudley and between the consul and his operatives. Forbes and Aspinwall then helped recruit more agents to assist Dudley in his investigations. When they sailed for home on June 30, they left £200 sterling (almost $1,000) with Dudley, in addition to the £500 (nearly $2,500) they had already given him, and promised to ask the State and Navy departments to provide him ongoing funds. Although these amounts seem meager, Maguire collected only £6–7 per week for himself and his assistants. Prior to this Dudley had paid detectives and witnesses from his own salary.[25]

With the extra money provided by Forbes and Aspinwall, Dudley paid Clarence Yonge, the former *Alabama* paymaster, a stipend to remain in England until the *Alexandra* trial concluded. The consul later extended this arrangement and retained Yonge as a witness against the ironclads. In addition to his testimony against the *Alexandra,* Yonge swore an affidavit connecting Bulloch to the Laird rams and James North to ironclad construction. Yonge related he had accompanied Bulloch to the Laird shipyard, made him a copy of the contract he and the Lairds had signed for the *Alabama,* and had seen drawings and specifications of ironclads the Lairds proposed building for Bulloch and the Confederacy. The affidavit continued that, upon returning to England, Yonge visited the Laird yard and saw the two ironclad rams building there and believed them to be the same as the drawings he had previously seen.[26]

Dudley also hired George Chapman, who had brought the consul Yonge's letters to his wife. Chapman had served with

Bulloch and Lieutenant Hamilton in the U.S. Navy and reestablished his relationship with them when he arrived in Liverpool. Neither Dudley nor Forbes completely trusted Chapman and were careful not to share any information that might be useful to the Confederates. Chapman gained entry into the Laird shipyard and furnished Dudley a detailed, but brief, description of the ironclads, which he estimated would be complete in about four months. Chapman believed they would "surpass anything afloat . . . for speed and invulnerability." He claimed to have seen the ships' blueprints, but he could not copy them or recall details because he had not wanted to arouse suspicion by studying the documents too closely. Dudley passed this information on to the State and Navy departments.[27]

In his expanded duties and responsibilities, Dudley traveled through northern England and Scotland instituting a system for preventing any additional Confederate "privateers or war ships" from sailing and "to adopt some plan to obtain evidence sufficient to stop the iron clad ram" building in Thomson's yard. Dudley hired several people throughout his new area of responsibility to observe shipyards and report any suspicious activity directly to him. He did not inform the other consuls that he had agents working in their districts, fearing the consuls would relax their own efforts if they knew someone else was investigating Confederate shipbuilding there. Dudley included in his report to Seward more detailed and accurate dimensions of Thomson's ironclad and expressed his hope and determination to obtain enough evidence to "arrest" it, although "there is in this, as in all other cases great difficulty in obtaining proof."[28]

Although Forbes, Aspinwall, and William Evarts, who helped with the *Alexandra* trial, all encouraged Dudley to present his evidence against the ironclads immediately, he and Minister Adams both agreed to wait until the ships launched before acting. He continued building his case, learning more and more details about the ironclads. But as the first launch date neared, he did not feel his evidence was very strong. His best witnesses, Yonge and Chapman, had been recently discredited during the *Alexandra* trial cross-examination. Dudley had also been forced to reveal the names not only of other informants, which ensured they would never work in Liverpool shipyards again, but his detectives, too, which rendered them useless for further investigation. He warned Seward, "It would therefore be well for the Department to consider at once, what is best to be done in the event of the government here refusing to stop these vessels, a contingency quite probable."[29]

Dudley again cautioned Secretary Seward of the ironclads' speed and invulnerability, doubting that any U.S. Navy ship could stop them or any American fortification could resist them. The builders had spared no pain or expense to make them the most "perfect and invulnerable" that "science or experience could suggest." Dudley had not been able to meet Chief Baron Pollock's criteria for proving the ships were built and "armed" in British waters. The consul urged the secretary to prepare to meet these "monsters" either on the ocean or "at our own sea ports."[30]

Number 294 launched on July 4, 1863, and it was now time for Dudley to present his evidence. But there was a new problem. One of the Lairds stated the day prior to the launch that the Emperor of China had originally ordered the ships, but they had been sold to the French government. To give credence to this story, number 294 launched as *El Tousson* flying an English flag on the stern and a French flag midship. This was Dudley's first indication of Mallory and Bulloch's "foolproof" plan to spirit the ironclads out of England. Still, the consul assured Seward he would make out the best case he could against the ship, but he doubted if he would succeed.[31]

Four months earlier, on March 9, Bulloch had received a letter from Secretary Mallory. Upon hearing Bulloch's doubts about getting the ironclads safely out of England, Mallory proposed an alternate construction plan. The secretary also had an idea for saving the Laird rams. First, he suggested Bulloch visit John Slidell, the Confederate emissary in Paris, to see about building ironclads in France. Mallory did not feel at liberty to explain, but he believed the French government would cooperate with the endeavor while not giving "formal assent." Mallory's suggestion evolved from a meeting between Slidell and Emperor Napoléon III, during which the emperor asked why the South did not use French shipyards to construct a navy and seemingly indicated he would not consider this as violating French neutrality. He even proposed building the ships ostensibly for the Italian government, to lessen suspicion. Napoléon soon retreated from this suggestion telling Slidell the "Italian plan" was too risky.[32]

A few months later, in early 1863, Lucien Arman—a leading shipbuilder, member of the Chamber of Deputies, and confidant of Napoléon III—asked Slidell if the Confederacy had any interest in building ships in France. Arman hinted the government might even allow the ships to be armed before sailing. Slidell felt certain Arman acted with Napoléon's blessing, and after some discussion the two agreed the builder would accept cotton bonds in payment, if the emperor did not object to their being sold in France. The new French secretary of foreign affairs, Edouard Drouyn de Lhuys, told Slidell "he was quite willing to close his eyes . . . until some direct appeal was made to him." Slidell also visited Eugène Rouher, the commerce minister, who did not object to the plan. Slidell, however, lacked the expertise and funds to initiate a shipbuilding program on his own, so he contacted Mallory who dispatched Bulloch to Paris in March 1863.

In Paris Bulloch met with Arman, who reassured him that the emperor and his foreign and commerce ministers approved the plan, the only requirement being the ships must sail under a neutral flag. Bulloch contracted with Arman for four clipper corvettes of 1,500-ton displacement with 400-horsepower engines. Arman would build two ships himself and subcontract with J. Voruz, a Nantes shipbuilder, for the other two. Arman told Bulloch the emperor had reviewed and approved their contract. Bulloch later contracted with Arman for two 172-foot ironclads.

A few weeks after Mallory proposed Bulloch begin building ships, including ironclads, in France, the secretary suggested Bulloch transfer ownership of the Laird rams to Arman, "a Member of the Corps Législatif, and who is said to have the confidence of the Emperor, is indicated as a party willing to receive the transfer and complete the outfit." Bulloch had already considered this idea, and during his visit with Slidell in March, Arman had introduced Bulloch to François and Adrien Bravay of Bravay and Company, a firm that had acted as purchasing agents for the Pasha of Egypt and other foreign governments.

For a commission, the Bravays agreed to buy the Laird rams, complete them to Bulloch's exact specifications, then resell them to him once they were beyond British jurisdiction. To add legitimacy to the transaction, the Bravays, coincidentally, had apparently agreed in December 1862 to secretly purchase two ironclads for the Pasha. Slidell received indications that the French government would support the Bravays' title if the British wanted assurance the vessels were intended for a neutral nation.

Bulloch realized that since Dudley suspected the Laird rams of being for the Confederacy, the sale must be able to withstand close scrutiny from the British officials. He again relied on his solicitor's counsel. Hull advised that all papers and letters relating to the contract must support and "tend to prove" the sale was legitimate. Also, since the courts would probably call the Lairds to testify, the builders must believe Bulloch had truly transferred title to the Bravays. Bulloch then wrote the Lairds a formal letter stating that British government interference with all ships suspected of being for the South had caused him to doubt that the ironclads could be completed without confiscation. To avoid this likelihood and the loss of time and money, Bulloch asked the Lairds to sell the ships for enough to ensure him a reasonable profit and to relieve him of further obligation under the contract. The Lairds agreed to handle the sale for a 2.5 percent commission. While Bulloch and the Bravays were negotiating a contract that Hull believed could stand up in British courts, the Russian government offered to buy the ships. Bulloch declined the offer, with the excuse that the Russians were friends of the North and they might be acting as Northern agents purchasing the vessels to use against the South. After Hull once again reviewed the contract, Bulloch signed the agreement transferring title for the rams to Bravay and Company on June 18, 1863. Hull then told Bulloch the rams could not be recovered by any process the Bravays "chose to resist." So the ships Dudley hoped to stop now legally belonged to a French company, not to Bulloch.[33]

Despite the rumored French ownership, Dudley moved ahead with his application to stop the ironclads. On July 7, 1863, the consul, his counsel Andrew T. Squarey, George Chapman, Clarence Yonge, William Russell, and Joseph Ellis appeared before Liverpool's collector of customs, Price Edwards, to present their evidence against the Laird rams. Dudley affirmed that the Lairds had previously built the *Alabama* for the Confederates and it was now committing hostilities against the United States. Chapman swore he had spoken privately with Bulloch, Lieutenant Hamilton, and Charles Prioleau who all admitted Bulloch was a Confederate agent, in Liverpool to buy warships. Chapman also told of visiting the Laird shipyard and seeing two ironclad vessels, which a local captain claimed were "without doubt for the Southerners." Yonge described Bulloch's relationship with the Confederacy, his responsibilities in Liverpool, and his role in the building and launching of the *Alabama*. The *Alabama*'s former paymaster also claimed to have seen plans in July 1862 for ironclads the Lairds proposed building for the Confederacy, and upon returning to Liverpool in April 1863 he saw two ironclads under construction in the Laird shipyard and he believed these were the same as the ones in the plans. Russell, a master mariner, and Ellis, a master shipwright, attested they had been present when number 294 launched and had examined her closely. They described the ship's iron plating and her "piercer" and concluded, "We have no hesitation in saying that the said vessel is an iron clad ram of the most formidable description and cannot be intended for any purpose but that of war."[34] This comprised the total "evidence" Dudley had amassed against the rams. Having to identify his witnesses and detectives during the *Alexandra* trial clearly hampered his efforts to find people willing and able to testify against the rams. Dudley then took his affidavits to Minister Adams, who relayed them to Lord Russell with a note expressing the danger to the relationship between their two countries inherent in such hostile acts by British subjects.[35]

Although Dudley hoped to stop the ironclads before they sailed, he warned Secretary Seward that "my efforts may fail, quite likely fail." If the ships did escape, they could cause the North "much mischief" since its navy had nothing "equal to these monsters" for "speed or invulnerability." "No pains or expense has been spared in their construction, everything has been done that science or experience could suggest to make them perfect and invulnerable."[36]

While doubting the British government would stop the iron-clads, Dudley continued gathering evidence against them. He presented Price Edwards with two more affidavits on July 15. John Brady, a boilermaker working for Lairds, stated he knew Bulloch and had often seen him conferring with the foreman responsible for building the ironclads. Austin Hand, a caulker for Lairds, also swore he saw Bulloch superintending the laying of the ironclads' keels. The consul undoubtedly had to promise them free passage and employment in America if they lost their jobs because of their affidavits. Dudley explained to Edwards these statements confirmed that Bulloch, "the well known agent of the so called Southern Confederacy," had overseen the ironclads' construction. But Edwards replied "unofficially" that Lairds had told the government the ships were for either Egypt or Turkey and that he "gave credence to what the Lairds said about them." The consul also passed these statements along to Adams, who sent them on to Russell. Despite reassurance from Evarts that he had reviewed the evidence and had "little doubt that the vessel will be stopped," Dudley reported to Seward that he believed the British government would accept the Lairds' explanation and do nothing.[37]

Union friend Richard Cobden, in a speech in Parliament, urged Palmerston to stop the Laird ironclads. The prime minister replied that the French consul had claimed one ironclad for the emperor of France. Dudley immediately contacted the French consul to verify Palmerston's statement. The French vice consul visited Dudley to personally assure him that no ironclads were building in England for the emperor. The French consul, however, declined to officially deny French ownership stating he did not wish to publicly call the prime minister a liar. The vice consul did acknowledge that he had attended a luncheon at Lairds at the invitation of a Mr. Bravay. At the luncheon Bravay had inquired about getting French papers for the ironclads. The vice consul explained the necessary formalities, but he had heard nothing further from either the Bravays or the Lairds. Dudley now understood how Bulloch expected to get the rams out of England.[38]

Dudley reported the conversation to both Seward and Adams and added that he had heard the "pretended sale" was simply a scheme to evade the Foreign Enlistment Act. The consul immediately began trying to prove the sale was not legitimate and asked Adams to contact William Dayton, the American minister in Paris. But Adams "sneered" down the idea and then went on an extended vacation in Scotland, out of contact with the legation. Dudley wrote Dayton on his own, on July 31, asking that he investigate to verify or repudiate the claim of French ownership. Dudley had no doubt the sale was a "sham" and a ruse to free the vessels to commit hostilities against the United States. Dayton contacted French foreign minister Drouyn de Lhuys, who promised "immediately to attend to it." Dayton assured Dudley on August 4 that he did not believe the French would allow their flag to be fraudulently used to get the rams to sea. Drouyn de Lhuys informed Dayton on August 15 that every French authority, including the emperor, denied the ironclads were building for their government. Dayton stressed the damage to Franco-American relations if the ironclads were to escape under the French flag. The foreign minister replied that if Dayton could supply evidence of the vessels' true ownership, he would have grounds to act against them. Dudley had anticipated the request and sent Dayton copies of his application and the supporting affidavits. On August 25, Drouyn de Lhuys wrote Bravay that since he claimed to have purchased the ironclads for the Pasha of Egypt, French officials had no authority to support him in getting them out of England. He would have to rely upon the Pasha for assistance. Drouyn de Lhuys sent Dayton copies of this correspondence, and the minister forwarded them to the American legation in London and to Dudley in Liverpool.[39]

Dudley had also written the American consul general at Alexandria, Egypt, in early August requesting that he contact the Egyptian government to learn if that country had purchased the ironclads. When there was no reply after three weeks, Dudley telegraphed the consul asking for a reply. The consul general wired back that the Egyptian government denied ordering any ironclad. With Adams away on vacation, the legation in London also sought to disprove Egyptian ownership. Benjamin Moran, the legation secretary, visited the Turkish ambassador, who thought it untrue. Charles Wilson, acting in Adams's stead, also telegraphed the consul general at Alexandria and learned that Egypt denied ownership.[40]

As Dudley worked to prove Bravay was not the ironclads' legitimate owner, the second vessel, number 295 (now christened *El Monassir*), launched on August 29. On September 1 the consul applied to Collector of Customs Edwards to stop her. Dudley included his affirmation, the affidavits of Chapman and Yonge previously submitted on number 294, a new statement from Ellis (who had given an affidavit against number 294), and one from an American master mariner, Charles Prentis, who confirmed number 295 could serve no other purpose than that of warship.[41]

When Adams returned from vacation on September 3, he realized that his earlier confidence that the British government would stop the ironclads might have been misplaced. He not only approved of his staff's and Dudley's actions but moved quickly to present the information they had gathered to Lord Russell, along with Dudley's evidence against number 295. Adams stressed the danger represented by these ships and concluded with "this last solemn protest against the commission of such an act of hostility against a friendly nation."[42] The next day Dudley presented Edwards with an affidavit by Thomas Sweeney, who worked in the Laird yard, along with a note stating number 294 had taken on coal and could slip away to sea at any moment. Meanwhile, on September 4, Adams received Russell's September 1 response to the request to stop number 294, stating that the government had no grounds for action, Dudley's "evidence" was mere hearsay, and the Crown's attorneys could find no flaw in the Bravays' title. Adams replied on September 5, in his strongest language yet, emphasizing that the first ironclad was nearly ready to sail "on its hostile errand against the United States" and the British government's refusal to act was "practically opening to the insurgents full liberty in this kingdom." The American minister concluded with his now well-known statement: "It would be superfluous in me to point out to your Lordship that this is war."[43] Adams confided to Dudley, who was in London, that war with Great Britain seemed inevitable.[44]

Lord Russell had closely followed the ironclads' progress and constantly solicited the Crown's law officers' opinions on stopping the vessels. After reviewing Dudley's first application, the legal experts advised Russell not to seize the ships. Price Edwards stated that the French consul had told him personally that the ships were French property and he would submit the required papers to secure her departure. Edwards, therefore, had "every reason" to be satisfied the two ironclads were not for the South, but for a Frenchman. He later added that the ships were built for a Paris banker on behalf of a foreign government, not the Confederacy. After receiving Dudley's letters disputing Edwards's account of the French consul claiming French ownership, Russell asked the Treasury officials to explain the discrepancy. In reply, Edwards said he could see no discrepancy between his account and that submitted by Dudley. Dissatisfied with this answer, on August 5, Russell submitted these letters to the law officers and asked if this new information would cause them to change their earlier opinion. They responded that although they did not consider Edwards's explanation to be satisfactory, Bravay claimed to be the ships' owner and acted in that capacity. There was considerable evidence that he was the true owner and no proof that he was not. The officers, therefore, again recommended the Crown take no action against the ships.

Russell remained unconvinced that the ships belonged to the Frenchman and not to the Confederacy. He asked the Treasury to continue their investigation and then telegraphed the British ambassador in Paris inquiring about French ownership. The ambassador responded that the French government had already declined to assist Bravay and had informed him that he would have to seek official support from Egypt. Russell then contacted Alexandria to inquire of the Egyptian government's interest in the ironclads. On August 31, Russell received Dudley's letter to Edwards stating that number 294 would leave either that night or the following night. Although this proved untrue, a second letter contained Prentis's affidavit stating that the ship could sail on very short notice. At this same time, the foreign secretary learned the second ironclad had launched on August 29. On August 31, a telegram informed Russell that Egypt's viceroy refused to accept the rams.

The following morning, September 1, the foreign secretary sent the Treasury and the Home Office a note, stating "that so much suspicion attached to the iron-clad vessels at Birkenhead that if sufficient evidence can be obtained to *lead to the belief* [emphasis added] that they are intended for the Confederate States of America, Lord Russell thinks the vessels ought to be detained until further examination can be made."[45] Obviously this represented a major shift in Russell's position from requiring positive legal proof of "arming, equipping and warlike intentions." This same day, however, he informed Adams that the British government had no legal basis for stopping number 294 since the law officers could find no flaw in the Bravay title.

Dudley's application to stop number 295 arrived the next day, followed by another affidavit affirming that number 294 could easily be put to sea. Russell decided to act that day, September 3. His office requested that the Treasury direct customs officials to stop the ironclads "as soon as there is reason to believe that they are actually about to put to sea, and to detain them until further orders."[46] Two days later he clarified his intent: the builders could continue construction, but the ships were not permitted to go "out for a trial run or any other pretext." Russell had detained the ironclads on his own authority. In explaining his actions to Prime Minister Palmerston, he wrote that the "conduct of the gentlemen who have contracted for the two iron clads is so very suspicious that I have thought it necessary to direct they should be detained." He had consulted the solicitor general, who agreed with the action "as one of policy though not of strict law." Russell felt that, even if they later had to release the ships, at least the British government had "satisfied the opinion, which prevails here as well as in America, that that kind of neutral hostility should not be allowed to go on without some attempt to stop it."[47] The foreign secretary then asked Palmerston to call a cabinet meeting to decide the best course to pursue if he disagreed with this decision. The prime minister gave at least tacit approval by not calling the meeting. He later informed Russell, "I think you are right in detaining the Ironclads now building on the Mersey, although the result may be that we shall be obliged to set them free. There can be no doubt that ships plated with Iron must be intended for warlike purposes, but to justify seizure we must . . . prove that they are intended for . . . the Confederates to employ against the Federal Government." This both men were well aware could prove difficult.[48]

Although Russell had decided on September 3 to stop the rams, at least temporarily, he did not immediately tell Adams or announce the move publicly. Adams's increasingly bellicose notes served only to irritate the foreign secretary and probably moved him to let the American minister stew a bit. Palmerston, ever aware of the political consequences of appearing to bow to foreign pressure, suggested Russell respond to Adams, in civil terms, "you be damned." Not until September 8 did Russell send a brief note informing Adams "instructions have been issued which will prevent the departure of the two Ironclad vessels at Liverpool."[49]

Dudley, meanwhile, continued trying to build a case against the rams. He inquired of Squarey, his attorney, if he believed their evidence sufficient or if there was anything else Dudley could do. Squarey replied that, if the authorities believed the affidavits, then the evidence was strong enough to justify seizure. The ironclads' warlike nature seemed "entirely conclusive." Their Confederacy connection, however, relied on Yonge's and Chapman's affidavits. Although cross-examination during the *Alexandra* trial had called their characters into question, there was nothing that questioned the truthfulness of their statements. Squarey, therefore, believed their evidence was "entitled to credit," and he could offer no suggestions to improve Dudley's case against the rams.[50]

Although relieved when he heard on September 8 that Russell had stopped the ironclads, Dudley soon learned that the restriction might be temporary. The official statement published on September 14 said "the two ironclad steamers . . . are not permitted to leave the Mersey until satisfactory evidence can be given of their destination, or at least until the inquiries which are now being prosecuted with a view to gain such evidence shall be brought to a conclusion."[51] Meanwhile, construction on the vessels continued apace, with two crews working around the clock on number 295. Furthermore, an agent reported that same morning that number 294 had taken on coal from midnight to 6 a.m. in preparation for a trial run, from which she would not return. Dudley immediately informed Price Edwards of this development and asked him to "prevent her from sailing." He also telegraphed Adams the disquieting news. The consul watched helplessly as the ironclad steamed out into the river, then traveled a short distance upstream, and entered a public dock.[52]

Adding to his anxiety, Dudley received news shortly before the 294 left her dock that sixty crew members from the *Florida* were on their way to Liverpool. When the crewmen arrived on September 12, the consul's men met their train from Cardiff and struck up conversation, hoping to discover if the sailors were to join the ironclad's crew. Although Dudley's operatives learned little, they did talk with a man who had a note from the *Florida*'s Captain Maffitt to Bulloch asking that he find other employment for the crew. Dudley's agent convinced the man to bring the note to the consulate, where Dudley had it copied. The copy accompanied Dudley's letter warning about the crew to Adams, who forwarded it to Russell. The foreign secretary had already read the news in local papers. The Earl of Derby was convinced that Dudley had placed the report in the papers to attract government attention, although this could not be confirmed. Fearing the Confederates might try to hijack the ironclad on its trial run, Russell altered the conditions for a run he had already approved. The ship could only go out if it carried enough British sailors and marines to prevent any forcible takeover. Faced with this alternative, the Lairds opted on September 14 to cancel the scheduled trial run.[53]

In the midst of this turbulence, a merchant "of first respectability" informed Dudley that the ironclads would try to escape under the Danish flag. Dudley visited the Danish consul who reported he knew nothing of such a plan and promised to tell Dudley if anything new developed. Dudley passed this on to Adams. The next day the Danish consul stated he had just received a letter from his minister in London instructing him to contact the Lairds about purchasing the rams. Dudley wrote the American minister in Copenhagen asking that he try to confirm the offer's validity. When Adams received Dudley's letter, he reacted with "Pshaw! . . . poor Dudley is nervous." Benjamin Moran confided to his diary, "it would not injure us if some of that nervousness could get possession of Mr. Adams for in that case he would be more inclined to attend to his affairs than now."[54] Moran, on his own initiative, visited the Danish minister and learned the minister had, indeed, asked his consul to purchase the rams, if they were for sale, for his country's use in defending its claim in Schleswig-Holstein. The Danish consul had not yet relayed Lairds' answer. By the following morning, Minister Adams had reconsidered his quick dismissal of Dudley's concern and asked Moran what he had learned from the Danish minister. After hearing Moran's report, Adams complimented Dudley on his vigilance. This incident ended when the Lairds refused to sell the ironclad.[55]

Although Foreign Secretary Russell oversaw the investigation into the rams, Prime Minister Palmerston closely followed the situation. On September 13, Palmerston wrote Russell that the Crown's law officers did not believe there were lawful grounds for detaining the ships. He also expressed concern that Bravay might sell them to the Confederates, the Northern government, or the French. None of these alternatives appealed to the prime minister, so he suggested purchasing the ironclads for the British Navy. Russell agreed and urged the Duke of Somerset to buy the ships. If the Bravays refused to sell, this would be "strong presumptive proof that they were already bought by the Confederates." After surveying the ships, the Royal Navy contacted the Lairds about making an offer. A short time later, the builders replied the owner would not sell the ironclads.[56]

Russell even instructed William Grey, the British embassy secretary in Paris, to contact Bravay directly. Bravay still refused to sell. This helped convince Russell that Bravay "is playing us false about the iron clads." The foreign secretary explained to Grey the importance of establishing the Confederacy as the rams' true destination, "supposing our conjecture is right." Grey had already established a relationship with Bravay's clerk, who sold him copies of Bravay's contracts purchasing the ships from Bulloch. By October 2, Palmerston could write Russell, "Somerset thinks that the Deed of Sale of these Ships from the Confederacy to Bravay was a deception and meant only as a cloak."[57]

When Russell issued the original detention order on September 1, Royal Navy Captain E. A. Inglefield moved the H.M.S. *Majestic* into place in the Mersey, near the Laird yard to ensure the rams did not leave. The H.M.S. *Liverpool* and three gunboats soon joined the *Majestic*. Inglefield also created an intelligence network to signal any movement by the ironclads. The Confederate seamen's arrival made the British captain even more wary and alert. When 294 began taking on coal and preparing for sea on October 6, Inglefield felt sure the Confederates were planning to "carry the vessel in question out of British waters by force." Two days later his spies reported a rumor that seemed to confirm his suspicions. He reported, "Have received private information. Number of Men are ready for secret service—tow lines placed on board." Inglefield then asked, "Shall I move 'Liverpool' or gunboat to the entrance of the Great Float?" Russell reacted immediately with orders to seize the ironclad "today" and then added a note to "seize" the 295 also. Inglefield moved gunboats alongside of both rams and placed marines on board to patrol the rams at night. Bulloch later called the thought of a Confederate scheme to forcibly take over the ironclads and move them from British waters "preposterous." Acting upon Foreign Office orders, Inglefield assumed "full possession" of the rams on October 30 and moved them to anchor adjacent to the *Majestic*.[58]

On October 10, Dudley informed Seward that Russell had ordered Captain Inglefield to seize the rams if either "attempted to sail." This action finally convinced Dudley that the British government was "now in earnest" about stopping the ironclads. Until then he had remained wary despite assurances the ships would not sail until British authorities were sure they would not be used against the United States. In Dudley's view, this left a loophole through which they could escape on "any decent pretext." He concluded his letter with "I think I can now say to you with every assurance of its truth that the two Rams are stopped."[59]

As the British built their case against the rams, Dudley aided the Crown's attorneys. He directed his own lawyers, Squarey and Lush, to assist in any way they could. At the prosecuting attorneys' suggestion, Dudley even traveled to Paris and tried without success to connect the Bravays to Bulloch or other Confederate agents. Dudley kept Yonge, Sweeney, and Hand on the payroll and had the State Department return Chapman from the United States so they could all be available for the trial.[60]

Even after the British seized the rams, Bulloch expected the English legal system would not sustain the action. Commander North, however, terminated his contract with Thomson by "mutual agreement" on December 21, 1863, and he sold the Clyde ironclad to Denmark. Both Bulloch and his solicitor, meanwhile, believed authorities would push for a speedy trial for the Laird rams and the court would free the ships based on Chief Baron Pollock's *Alexandra* decision. To Bulloch's surprise and disappointment, the government did not immediately set a trial date and he could do nothing but wait. The British government finally scheduled the trial for May 1864. Bulloch concluded that Lord Russell would never permit the ironclads to sail unless Emperor Napoléon interceded on Bravay's behalf as a French citizen. Either Bulloch had not learned that France had already refused to support Bravay's claim or he thought the emperor might change his mind. On January 27, 1864, Bulloch journeyed to France to have Bravay appeal directly to Emperor Napoléon. The emperor's emissary informed Bravay and Slidell that Napoléon could not ask the British to release the rams, although he hoped the Confederates would succeed in obtaining them. Bulloch, Slidell, Mason, and Captain Samuel Barron, the South's ranking naval officer in Europe, conferred and decided to sell the rams and recover whatever money possible to use for more promising projects.[61]

Bulloch immediately arranged with Bravay to sell the vessels for £210,000 sterling in completed condition or £182,000 in their current state. Bravay opened negotiations with the British government. Again slow communication between the South and Bulloch delayed and often confused the process, but in May 1864 the British purchased the rams in a "completed state" for £220,000 sterling; £29,000 went to the Lairds to complete construction and the Bravays received the remaining £191,000, of which £188,000 they passed on to Bulloch. Bulloch later wrote Mallory that selling the rams caused him "greater pain and regret than I ever thought it possible to feel."[62]

The British renamed the ironclads the *Scorpion* and the *Wivern*. The Royal Navy found the *Wivern* to be unsafe in the ocean as she "rolled 18 to 20 degrees, often had her decks awash, and in heavy swells her hull was almost completely hidden from observers in other ships." Her crew was "extremely wet and uncomfortable." The *Scorpion*, although an "identical" sister ship, proved "buoyant and steady" when "laid broadside on with the sea on her quarter."[63] While of questionable value on open seas, the ironclads probably would have performed well along Confederate coasts and harbors. Years later Bulloch still believed the rams "would have had no difficulty in running down any 'Monitor' then afloat, and I confidently believe that they would have broken up the blockade completely."[64] Without the Laird ironclads, Mallory's only hope for breaking the blockade now rested across the English Channel in France, where both Bulloch and Dudley next turned their attention.

OTHER CRUISERS
AND IRONCLADS

6

While focusing most of his attention on the Laird ironclads, Dudley kept watch for other possible Confederate warships. Bulloch, frustrated that British law had not protected his shipbuilding in England, felt compelled to seek help in France. But other Confederate agents using different methods for building and purchasing warships tested the U.S. consul.

In late April 1863, armed with new authority and additional money from Forbes and Aspinwall, Thomas Dudley toured northern England and Scotland searching for suspicious vessels. While in Glasgow checking the Thomson Brothers' shipyard for progress on North's ironclad, Dudley discovered a "screw steamer of about 1500 tons . . . with very fine lines capable of great speed." Her frame was "strong angle iron" covered by teak planking. Talking with the workers there convinced him the Thomsons were building the ship for the Confederates. Since it would be six months before the ship could launch, Dudley turned his attention to more immediate matters.[1]

The "screw steamer," called first the *Canton* and then the *Pampero*, had been under construction since October 1862. Secretary Mallory had sent Lieutenant George T. Sinclair to Great Britain earlier that year to build or buy "a clipper propeller for cruising purposes" and command her when she sailed. Upon reaching Liverpool, Sinclair immediately contacted Bulloch, who had instructions to provide help and money for the project. Based on Bulloch's experience, Sinclair learned he would be unable to buy a suitable ship, so he must have one built. Other projects had already drained Bulloch's finances so he had no money to share, but he could help Sinclair with copies of the *Alabama*'s contract and plans to serve as guidelines.[2]

Through his old friend James North, Sinclair eventually met the Thomsons, who agreed to build a larger version of the *Alabama*. Having no funds to secure the contract, Sinclair devised a most creative plan. After conferring with James Mason, the South's diplomatic agent in England, Sinclair decided to pay for his ship with bonds backed by Southern cotton. He struck a deal to furnish W. S. Lindsay and Company, a large shipbuilding firm headed by a pro-Southern member of Parliament, with 246 cotton bonds, each redeemable for 12,500 pounds of cotton delivered at any Confederate port within thirty days of demand. With cotton currently selling at eight cents a pound, the face value for 246 bonds was $246,000 or £51,250 sterling. Lindsay then contracted with the Thomsons to build the ship for £46,600 sterling. Lindsay would sell the bonds and pay the builders as the work progressed, the £4,650 sterling difference would be his profit. Lindsay distanced himself from the transaction by directing payment through Patrick Henderson and Company, one of seven investors who legally owned the vessel during construction. Edward Pembroke (either Henderson's partner or an agent) signed the construction contract and paid the Thomsons. Sinclair's name appeared nowhere in the contract, although he did move to Glasgow to oversee construction. The investors would transfer title to him when the *Pampero* was ready to sail.[3]

At 231 feet, the *Pampero* measured 21 feet longer than the *Alabama*. Like her older sister, she sported a powerful steam engine and a screw propeller. Under favorable winds she could spread the sails on her three bark-rigged masts, retract the propeller, and outrun most other vessels afloat. Unlike the *Alabama,* the *Pampero* incorporated composite construction with an iron frame and wood and iron planking. Composite construction decreased her weight, increased her strength, enlarged the cargo space, and with copper covering her bottom reduced fouling, a serious problem for iron ships operating in warm waters.[4]

If the Thomsons had completed the *Pampero* by June 1863, as the contract stated, she probably would have escaped before Dudley had time to build a case against her. Labor problems, however, hampered progress and Sinclair began to fear the British might seize his ship. He consulted with John Slidell in Paris where they considered transferring the ship to either French or German ownership, but neither alternative proved viable. Sinclair then suggested arming the ship in a French port, but Slidell vetoed the proposal, believing this might undermine the Laird ironclads' escape plan. Eventually the two Confederates reverted to an earlier plan to disguise her as a merchant ship, advertise for freight to carry to a foreign port, then place the crew and guns on board at "some intermediate point" after she escaped British waters. When the British government seized the *Alexandra,* Slidell, Sinclair, and the builders agreed to slow construction while awaiting the trial's final outcome.[5]

While they were waiting the *Pampero* caught Dudley's eye, however. He visited Glasgow again in August and noted her iron planking above and wood planking below the waterline and her "very powerful" engines, which the Thomsons were also building. Although the Thomsons claimed the Turkish government had ordered the ship, workmen told Dudley she was meant for the Confederacy. When he returned in September he became even more convinced of the ship's true nature and destination.[6]

Before leaving Glasgow, Dudley hired John Comb to gather evidence against the *Pampero.* Comb, as part owner of a ship under construction at Thomsons, had easy access to the boatyard. He soon reported the *Pampero* carried rigging similar to the *Alabama*'s, the Patrick Henderson Company made the payments for her, and Sinclair supervised her construction. Although Dudley considered this adequate proof that *Pampero* was a Confederate warship, the U.S. consul in Glasgow, Warren L. Underwood, disagreed and thought her a merchant ship. When workmen began removing any warlike features and adding a forecastle and a small deck cabin, in keeping with Sinclair's escape plan to disguise her as a commercial vessel, Underwood felt sure he was correct. Dudley, meanwhile, learned from a former foreman in the yard that the *Pampero* was a Confederate ship and she would carry sixteen guns. Comb then reported to Dudley that the workmen had rigged the gun tackle and were preparing to launch her, but surprisingly they had planked over the gun ports.[7]

The evidence Dudley compiled finally convinced Underwood in early October that this was indeed a Confederate warship. Underwood asked Dudley to return to Glasgow with Neil Black, one of his agents, as the ship would launch that week. Dudley immediately took the train to Glasgow and saw the *Pampero's* hull was finished and her masts and rigging were in place. Workmen were also busy closing the gun ports and removing shot lockers, magazines, and so on, which might reveal her true purpose. Although he had no doubt about the ship's nature or destination, Dudley feared British authorities might accept the ruse. Even if he convinced them this was a warship, he had no proof she belonged to the Confederacy. He telegraphed for two of his detectives to join him in Glasgow.[8]

Glasgow, like Liverpool, benefited from commercial ties with the Confederacy, and most residents favored the South. Local shipbuilders and shipyard workers refused to discuss the *Pampero's* true destination, and those who did would not give affidavits for fear they would lose their jobs and be blacklisted. Anxious, but lacking credible evidence, Underwood wrote of his suspicions to Minister Adams, who forwarded the letter to Lord Russell. The foreign secretary asked local customs officials to investigate. They reported that nothing on board the ship confirmed she was a warship, but she could easily be converted into one. Dudley then sent John Latham, who had sailed aboard the *Alabama* but later deserted, to Glasgow. Latham, mingling with the workmen, confirmed that the *Pampero's* construction and equipment suited a warship, not a commercial vessel, and that North and Sinclair had overseen her construction. He also reported that workmen had indeed removed the 150 crew lockers, but they had stowed them below for later use. A merchant ship would not sail with 150 crewmen and, therefore, would have no need for so many lockers.[9]

Despite their best efforts, Dudley and Underwood could uncover little damning evidence against the *Pampero*. After she launched on October 29, they knew they had to move quickly with what they had. Acting on Dudley's advice, Underwood and his attorney, Adam Patterson, on November 10 requested the Glasgow collector of customs to detain the ship. They submitted affidavits from Dudley, Underwood, Latham, two Thomson employees, and a merchant-ship broker. The six statements described the vessel's warlike characteristics, but no one could link her directly to the Confederacy. Dudley admitted, in a letter to Secretary Seward, that the affidavits "show her to be built as a war vessel . . . [but] the evidence that she is for the Confederates is entirely circumstantial and hearsay." Underwood forwarded copies to Adams, who sent them on to the Foreign Office. Underwood also induced the Glasgow Emancipation Society to petition Russell to stop the ship.[10]

Sinclair, either through intuition or information from other sources, realized that Northern agents were conspiring against his ship and contacted Commodore Samuel Barron, the Confederates' senior naval officer in Paris. Barron feared Sinclair might be called to testify if the British government seized the *Pampero* and advised that he gather all his documents relating to the transaction and bring them to Paris. Sinclair immediately left for the Continent.[11]

A few days later, on November 21, the British moored the gunboat *Bullfinch* in the Clyde, abreast of the *Pampero,* and posted a customs official on board. Although British officials now watched the ship constantly to prevent her escape, they had not seized her. On November 23, the collector of customs and the procurator fiscal assured Underwood he had proved his case. But neither he nor Dudley felt confident. Underwood gathered four additional affidavits and Dudley spent nearly £500 sterling in a futile attempt to connect the ship to the Confederacy. In early December, Lord Russell told Minister Adams that the Crown's law officers "had pretty much come to the conclusion to sustain proceedings against the . . . *Pampero*."[12]

Unlike previous cases, the collector of customs and Scottish legal officials actively investigated the *Pampero*'s ownership and original contracts. They learned only that Patrick Henderson Company of Glasgow had contracted for her as agents for E. Pembroke of London. George Thomson stated she was not intended as a warship and not meant for either American belligerent, but he declined to elaborate further. As the investigation proceeded, the Crown learned that James Galbraith of the Patrick Henderson Company admitted to being a part owner of the vessel. The lord advocate directed Galbraith to answer questions concerning the ship and to produce all documents pertinent to the transaction. Galbraith readily admitted Pembroke, representing the seven owners, contracted with Thomson to build the *Pampero* and that same day agreed to sell the ship to Sinclair, "who represented himself as a subject of the so-called Confederate States of America."[13]

Galbraith further stated that on October 21, 1863, Sinclair, fearing the British would seize the ship, cancelled the purchase contract and demanded return of the cotton bonds. Pembroke refused to turn the certificates over, so Sinclair had lost his investment. The lord advocate ruled the alleged cancellation did not negate the violation of the Foreign Enlistment Act. Officials seized the *Pampero* on December 10, 1863. Dudley worked closely with the Crown's lawyers building their case. As the April 5, 1864, trial date approached, the seven owners offered to sell the ship to the Royal Navy, but navy officials considered her unfit for service. The owners next proposed to make any alterations needed to guarantee she would be used only for commercial purposes. The lord advocate determined the government had proved its case, but the owners could keep the ship if they made the suggested changes to her structure, gave bond that she would be used only for peaceful purposes, and changed the registry to guarantee against transferring ownership. Dudley must have felt gratified not only at stopping the *Pampero* but also at the shift in the British government's attitude toward Confederate shipbuilding in their country. There were, however, still other Confederate agents and other Confederate ships demanding his attention.[14]

Earlier, Confederate Navy Secretary Mallory had dispatched another agent to England to seek suitable commerce raiders. Commander Matthew F. Maury, author of the internationally acclaimed *Wind and Current Chart of the North Atlantic* and *Explanations and Sailing Directions to Accompany the Wind and Current Charts,* which the world's sea captains depended upon, arrived in Liverpool with his thirteen-year-old son, Matthew, on November 23, 1862. A crippling injury early in his career had left Maury with a pronounced limp and kept him from sea duty, so he had spent the previous year and a half experimenting with electric mines and meddling in Confederate politics. Dudley reported Maury's arrival but failed to realize his purpose. Maury immediately visited Fraser, Trenholm and Company where he met Bulloch for the first time. Mallory had alerted Bulloch that Maury was coming and instructed him to pay Maury's living expenses. Bulloch later reported that Maury's mission was to investigate mines, torpedoes, magnetic exploders, and other underwater defensive devices. Mallory had also authorized Maury to buy and launch commerce raiders if that proved practical.[15]

After a few days in Liverpool, Maury and his son moved into modest rooms in London. A stream of scientists and sailors came to see him, many of whom he had already met in 1853 when he organized the International Maritime Meteorological Conference in Brussels and, as a U.S. Navy lieutenant, gave the opening address. Dutch Navy Captain Marin H. Jansen, who had attended the conference and had corresponded with Maury ever since, was in London on official business and dropped in on his old friend. Jansen offered to help Maury any way he could and Maury quickly accepted. Jansen would be visiting British shipyards in the course of his business, and Maury asked if he would "note every vessel that they have in progress [including warships and ironclads] . . . [h]er size and draft and fitness for armaments. She should not be over 15 ft. draft—good under canvas, fast under steam—with the ability to keep to sea for a year—using steam only when necessary."[16] When Jansen found a ship fitting these conditions, he was to drop Maury "a line." Maury's international renown provided the perfect cover, and even though Dudley quickly learned Maury had "made contracts" or was "about to make contracts for two or three other vessels for the south," the consul could learn no "particulars."[17]

Jansen soon compiled a list of possibilities. Maury requested money from Mallory, and Lieutenant William Lewis Maury, a distant cousin, arrived around February 1, 1863, with $1.5 million in cotton certificates. Although Maury could not sell them immediately, as John Slidell was negotiating the $15 million Erlanger loan and he did not want anything to jeopardize this, Maury deposited the certificates in a commercial bank and borrowed the needed funds against them. Another cousin in Liverpool, Thomas Bold, helped arrange the loan and then used the money to purchase the *Japan,* a merchant vessel under construction in Dumbarton, Scotland, in his own name. Neither Matthew Maury nor his cousin William, who was to be the ship's captain, approached the *Japan* in Dumbarton. Jansen prepared the ship for sea and earned "A thousand thanks" from Maury.[18]

The *Japan* had not escaped Glasgow consul Warren Underwood's notice. He attended the January launching, when Commander James North's daughter christened her *Virginia*. But Underwood assumed she was a blockade runner and not a warship. After being inspected and cleared by local customs officials, the *Japan* sailed on April 1, 1863. Like Bulloch, Maury shipped the guns, munitions, supplies, and extra crewmen (including his cousin) separately aboard the *Alar*. Observers recalled a "rather lame" man supervising the loading. The two ships met off the French coast near Brest. After five days of hard work, the guns were in place, the supplies stored, and the crew, consisting of British sailors from the *Japan* and the *Alar* and Confederate officers originally intended for the *Alexandra,* prepared to sail aboard the newly commissioned C.S.S. *Georgia.*[19]

Since the *Georgia* was originally built as a commercial vessel and no Southerner visited her or contracted for her, Dudley had no opportunity to stop her before she sailed. But he immediately accepted Underwood's assessment that she was a Confederate vessel and began gathering evidence against her in anticipation of later bringing suit. Two of his agents, Neil Black and J. Baxter Langley, were at Dumbarton when she sailed as the *Japan*. After talking with workmen and crewmen, both believed she was a Southern ship. Black even managed to get on board but found no armament and could not learn her destination. Dudley soon contacted two men who had sailed on the *Japan* but refused to enlist in the Confederate Navy. He obtained their affidavits, which implicated Thomas Bold as the person who fitted out the ship and his employer, Jones and Company of Liverpool, as the firm that furnished the crew.[20]

The *Georgia* left Brest on April 9, 1863, and took her first prize sixteen days later. Six and a half months later, she sailed into Cherbourg, France. During her cruise, she had captured and burned four prizes and released five others under bond, which meant their owners were obligated to pay the Confederate government the equivalent of the ship and cargo's value at war's end. Built as a merchant ship, the *Georgia* lacked the features necessary for an effective commerce raider, however. Her fixed propeller and small sail capacity made her slow and inefficient when under wind power alone. She could only give chase under steam, which meant frequent stops to reload with coal, and frequent recoaling put her in danger of violating British neutrality. Either Commander Maury's perceived need for secrecy or his ego had kept him from consulting with Bulloch, who could have told him the *Japan* would not make a suitable commerce raider. Upon landing at Cherbourg, Lieutenant Maury traveled to Paris and informed Commodore Barron of the *Georgia*'s shortcomings. Then he asked to be relieved of command because of ill health. Lieutenant William E. Evans, who had sailed with Maury, assumed command and oversaw the needed repairs. After about four months in port, the *Georgia* sailed "on a short cruise," for "special service," according to Bulloch. She apparently could not accomplish her unspecified mission and soon returned to France, reaching Pauillac on March 25, 1864.[21]

While the *Georgia* was still at sea, Dudley acquired a letter from a crewman, John Stanley, to his wife, who confirmed that she and the other wives regularly received half their husbands' monthly wages from Jones and Company. When the *Georgia* put into Cherbourg for repairs in October, Lieutenant Maury granted some crewmen leave, and several returned to Liverpool. Through Matthew Maguire, Dudley met Stanley, Francis Glassbrook, and

Benjamin Conolly. All three gave affidavits describing how they had been hired and paid by Jones and Company and their experiences aboard the *Georgia*. Dudley hired the three to stay in Liverpool and be available, if called upon to testify. He paid the same rate they had received aboard the *Georgia*.[22]

Maury's success in getting the *Georgia* to sea convinced Secretary Mallory to use him to purchase another vessel. Again, Maury avoided visiting shipyards himself. Instead, he sent Lieutenant William F. Carter to examine any available ships around London. Carter recommended buying the former H.M.S. *Victor*, a screw steamer the Royal Navy had used as a dispatch vessel. Her twin 350-horsepower engines promised good speed under steam and she carried six 24-pound guns. Although she looked promising, closer scrutiny would have revealed that her limited sails were too small to propel her under wind power alone and her limited coal capacity was inadequate for more than four days' sailing under steam. The Royal Navy used her as a coastal vessel, not for sea cruising. Worse still, the navy had condemned her, and an agent for the Chinese government previously declined to purchase her because "she was rotten."[23]

An agent for Maury's cousin Thomas Bold paid the Admiralty £9,375 sterling (approximately $45,750) for the *Victor* on September 14, 1863. The British government apparently did not realize it had sold a warship to the Confederate government. In fact, the newly renamed *Scylla* remained in the Royal Navy shipyard at Sheerness for a badly needed major overhaul to make her seaworthy. Because Dudley's area of responsibility did not include London, he was not involved in determining the ship's ownership or in trying to stop her. London consul Freeman Morse, however, became suspicious of the ship and alerted Minister Adams. They decided to gather more evidence before requesting detention. London customs officials, meanwhile, inspected her immediately without waiting for the American complaint. The inspectors found nothing suspicious about the *Scylla* or its new owners. The sudden inquiry alarmed Maury, however, and he ordered the ship to sea the following day to avoid seizure. She sailed so suddenly at midnight on November 24, 1863, that fifteen surprised British workmen were still on board.

Lieutenant William P. A. Campbell boarded the *Scylla* in the English Channel and commissioned her the C.S.S. *Rappahannock*. Campbell quickly realized his new command was "unseaworthy," and he put her into port at Calais, France, and applied to the French to use a local shipyard for repairs. U.S. minister to France William Dayton, backed by Secretary Seward, protested that the ship had not suffered damage at sea but had arrived in France in the same condition she had departed Britain. According to maritime law, a belligerent could not use a neutral port to improve a warship or increase crew size. Dayton presented evidence that the *Rappahannock* would be used to destroy Union merchant ships and promised the United States would hold France responsible for any damage she caused, if she escaped.

Commodore Barron, who had promised Secretary Mallory to get another commerce raider active against Union shipping, planned to decommission the ineffective *Georgia* and transfer her guns to the *Rappahannock*. She would then join the *Florida* in raiding Northern commerce or even coastal cities. Although Campbell completed some repairs to his ship, she was still unfit to sail. Also, he only had thirty-five crewmen aboard when he entered port, nearly half of whom were British Navy employees. But with Dayton closely scrutinizing developments, French authorities would not let Campbell add to his crew. Campbell, therefore, could neither complete the needed repairs nor fill out his crew. Barron stubbornly refused to acknowledge the futility of the situation and continued to press Campbell to get his ship seaworthy. Campbell's protests only elicited instructions from Barron to sail "when the *Rappahannock* was ready for sea" and rendezvous with the *Georgia*, take any needed armament and munitions, then "proceed to cruise against the enemy's commerce."[24]

French authorities, meanwhile, ordered both the *Georgia* and the *Florida* to leave port within twenty-four hours. The customs official also informed Lieutenant Campbell that if the *Rappahannock* did not sail soon she would be detained, possibly until the end of the war. The other two ships complied with the orders, but the *Rappahannock* had neither enough crewmen nor sufficient coal to sail. Foreign minister Drouyn de Lhuys then ordered port officials to prevent her from sailing without the minister of marine's permission. Slidell reprimanded Campbell for not sailing; Commodore Barron appointed Lieutenant Charles M. Fauntleroy to replace Campbell on March 21. Slidell believed he could circumvent Drouyn de Lhuys and appeal directly to Emperor Napoléon III, but the emperor would not intercede, and French authorities refused to release the *Rappahannock*. Lieutenant Fauntleroy must have been relieved as he had already informed Barron of the ship's many defects, and his crew had dwindled to twelve. He concluded his report by telling the commodore, "If a board of officers . . . had looked at the vessel earlier she would never have been in our hands today."

Without ever visiting the *Rappahannock,* Barron remained adamant that she sail. He pressed Slidell, who continued the campaign to have the ship released. Barron even ordered Lieutenant Evans to meet with Fauntleroy and arrange to transfer the *Georgia*'s guns to the *Rappahannock.* Evans met with Fauntleroy, but international law, enforced by French authorities, prevented any increase in the *Rappahannock*'s armament. Furthermore, upon seeing the *Georgia*'s battery, Fauntleroy realized she had only one gun he might use. Bulloch, meanwhile, learned enough of the *Rappahannock*'s condition and situation to recommend that Barron sell the ship; Barron, resenting the intrusion on his authority, refused. The stalemate continued with the ship sitting in Calais, deteriorating further.

The *Georgia,* after a short stay at Pauillac, moved on to Bordeaux, where she remained until April 28, 1863. Unable to transfer the *Georgia*'s guns or crew to the *Rappahannock* and convinced the *Georgia* could no longer serve the Confederacy, Barron turned her over to Bulloch to sell. The *Georgia* reached Liverpool on May 2, and Edward Bates, a Liverpool shipowner and Southern sympathizer, bought her on June 1. After removing "every vestige of war fittings," Bates chartered her to the Portuguese government and sailed for Lisbon on August 8. The United States, however, did not consider the sale legitimate, and the U.S.S. *Niagara,* waiting in international waters, captured the *Georgia,* put a prize crew on board, and sailed her to the United States, where a prize court condemned her and sold her to the highest bidder.[25]

One reason Bulloch did not want Slidell and Barron to persist in pressing France to free the *Rappahannock* was that he still hoped to acquire one of the ironclads Lucien Arman had built in France, and he feared wrangling with the authorities would interfere. Bulloch had originally selected England over France for shipbuilding because he believed he could operate under English law more easily than if he subjected his efforts to the whims of Emperor Napoléon III. Arman had approached Slidell in early 1863, assuring him that the emperor supported Confederate shipbuilding in France. When Slidell asked for Foreign Minister Drouyn de Lhuys's approval, the minister replied, "It is better that I know nothing of it. I am quite willing to close my eyes to it until some direct appeal is made to me."[26] By mid-March Bulloch had begun to doubt the English would allow the Laird rams to sail. So he visited Paris and contracted with Arman for four corvettes and later, on July 16, for two ironclads. Arman would build two corvettes and the ironclads in his shipyard at Bordeaux. Since Bulloch wanted the ships as soon as possible, Arman contracted with J. Voruz of Nantes to build the other two cruisers. Although these projects were outside Dudley's purview, he heard of Confederate shipbuilding in France and asked American minister William Dayton about it in August 1863. Dayton assured him there was "a wholesale system of lying on both sides of the channel" and there was no reason for concern.[27]

Before Bulloch signed the contract for the ironclads, Slidell visited Emperor Napoléon III to obtain his assurance that the French government would not interfere with the ironclads' construction or sailing. Napoléon replied, "You may build the ships, but it will be necessary that their destination be concealed."[28] This satisfied both Slidell and Bulloch, and they felt confident the South would soon have sufficient naval power to break the Northern blockade. Rumors soon circulated that Arman and Voruz were building Confederate ships. Arman spread the word that a merchant had ordered the corvettes for the China-Japan trade and the two ironclads belonged to Egypt's pasha. In early September 1863 John Bigelow, the U.S. consul in Paris, investigated but concluded the rumors of Confederate shipbuilding were not true.[29]

The great likelihood of Southern success in getting the French-built ships to sea changed on September 9 when Trémont, Voruz's confidential correspondence clerk, called on Minister Dayton and offered to furnish proof of Confederate shipbuilding at Bordeaux and Nantes. Dayton, wanting to give himself plausible deniability for dealing with a person selling his employer's secrets, referred Trémont to Bigelow. Trémont's extensive knowledge of the ships' dimensions, costs, and other details convinced Bigelow the Frenchman was telling the truth. According to Trémont, the ships would be ready in three months. He explained the builders had obtained government permission to construct the six ships and to arm the four corvettes through "fraudulent representations."[30] If the French authorities learned the truth, the ships would not be allowed to sail. Trémont showed Bigelow some original documents and letters and said he would return in two days with even more evidence confirming the relationship between the builders and the Confederates. Since he would be subject to some expense and risk, Trémont asked for 20,000 francs payable when his information prevented the ships from being delivered to the South. The frugal Bigelow bargained him down to 15,000 francs for this invaluable information.

Trémont produced ten documents, including three letters between Arman and Voruz and from Voruz to his son describing the ships as being built for the Confederacy. Although Arman claimed the ironclads would not be armed in France, other letters confirmed they would be. Taken together, the papers proved Arman had lied about the ships' ownership and had fraudulently obtained permission to build them in violation of French neutrality. Trémont furnished the damning information believing no French official was involved in the cover-up. Dayton overtly accepted this assumption, though he suspected French government complicity. The American minister maintained this pretense even when it later became apparent that French officials had indeed been aware. When Dayton presented this evidence to Foreign Minister Drouyn de Lhuys, the minister expressed shock and denied "any knowledge of anything of this kind."[31]

Both Dayton and Bulloch believed the French government would act according to its interests and not rely on legal precedent. Dayton concluded, "As to what the law may be it does not, I apprehend, much matter."[32] If the French intended to maintain good relations with the Northern government, they would stop the ships or at least prevent the builders from arming them. Bulloch expressed a similar opinion to Secretary Mallory: "My belief is, that the construction of the ships will not be interfered with, but whether they will be allowed to leave France or not will depend upon the position of affairs in America at the time of their completion."[33] Indeed, both Dayton and Bulloch were correct: French actions depended not only on success or failure of Union or Confederate armies but also on the progress of the French conquest of Mexico and the government established by Napoléon III's nephew Maximilian. In the end, Drouyn de Lhuys concluded that French national interests necessitated he continue a policy of neutrality. In mid-November 1863, he called in Arman and Voruz and told them they must find legitimate third-party buyers or they could not complete their ships. By late December, the French minister assured Dayton that the builders were looking for new buyers, which satisfied Dayton for the time being. When Dudley visited Paris on December 18, 1863, to investigate the rumored Confederate shipbuilding, Dayton was ill and Bigelow was away. So Dudley learned surprisingly little.[34]

Construction on the vessels, meanwhile, resumed. In January 1864, Bulloch met with Slidell, Mason, and Barron in Paris to discuss their options. Determined to salvage at least some ships, they decided to keep the cruisers and sell the ironclads. Both Slidell and Arman still believed Napoléon III would countermand Drouyn de Lhuys's orders and allow the ships to sail. Much to their chagrin, the emperor would not intercede. In fact, when Arman visited Napoléon, the emperor threatened to imprison him and seize his ships if he did not sell them at once to a bona fide buyer. Voruz acted quickly, sold his two corvettes to Peru, and settled his accounts with Bulloch. Arman, however, secretly proposed to Bulloch a scheme whereby the Frenchman would ostensibly sell one ironclad to a Danish banker, with the stipulation that he resell it to Bulloch once it cleared French jurisdiction. Bulloch declined, believing "This would simply be substituting France for England, and then Denmark for France . . . and if the two most powerful maritime nations in the world have not been able to resist the importunities of the United States, it would be simply absurd to hope for success through the medium of Denmark, a weak Power at best."[35] Arman then, through subterfuge and in violation of French neutrality, delivered three ships (two corvettes and one ironclad) to Prussia, a country then at war with Denmark. Dayton protested, fearing the vessels would eventually reach the South, and Drouyn de Lhuys delayed delivery until the Prussian-Danish War was already decided.[36]

In August 1864, Bulloch signed a release terminating his contract with Arman, but the two continued corresponding. Arman still held out the possibility of delivering an ironclad to the Confederates. He had agreed in June to sell the second ironclad to Denmark through a Swedish banker, but Dayton's protests and other difficulties delayed delivery until the Danish-Prussian War had ended. So when Arman applied for permission to deliver the ship, Drouyn de Lhuys learned of the ruse but agreed anyway, since a sale to Denmark no longer violated French neutrality. Renamed the *Staerkodder*, the former *Sphinx* left Bordeaux on October 15, 1864, and sailed directly to Copenhagen, although she had cleared for Helsingborg, Sweden. In Copenhagen Danish officials rejected the ship based on her late delivery. Arman's agent Henri de Rivière then offered the ship to Bulloch. The Danes had directed that Arman alter the ship to fit their needs when they originally agreed to purchase the vessel. Bulloch sent Captain Eugène Tessier, a trusted agent, to Copenhagen to inspect the ironclad. Tessier reported she showed "no sign of weakness," but the alterations had limited her fittings. With this information and the knowledge the ship was "clear of French interference," Bulloch signed a new contract on December 16, 1864, to pay de Rivière 375,000 francs (or about $75,000) for the ironclad.[37]

At Bulloch's request for a captain, Commander Barron appointed Captain Thomas Jefferson Page and suggested he might lift the blockade at Wilmington, North Carolina, intercept California steamers, attack New England ports, and destroy U.S. fisheries. Bulloch, meanwhile, arranged for the ship's arms, supplies, and crew. He convinced the *City of Richmond's* owners to delay their ship's run through the blockade to carry the ironclad's crew to meet their ship. The ironclad, now called the *Olinde,* left Copenhagen on January 7, 1865, and, despite a severe winter storm that forced her to seek refuge in Danish and Norwegian ports, reached the rendezvous point, the small French island of Houat, on January 24. Bulloch's choosing a French island seems confusing since he had so much trouble getting the ship from under that government's control in the first place. At Houat, Page, who had sailed aboard the vessel as a passenger from Copenhagen, supervised the transfer of the crew and provisions from the *City of Richmond* and then commissioned his vessel the C.S.S. *Stonewall,* a name "not inconsistent with her character and one which will appeal to the feelings and sympathies of our people at home," on January 25. The *Stonewall* sailed from France on January 28, 1865.[38]

Although Bulloch must have realized the South had slim chances of independence at this point, he believed that news of a Confederate ironclad coming would "animate the spirits of the Southern people." He hoped, also, that "the exaggerated rumours of her power and efficiency" would force the North to delay its attack on the sole remaining serviceable Southern port at Wilmington, North Carolina. Preparations to defend against the ironclad could possibly cause the North confusion and delay the impending attack on the port.[39]

Dudley learned the Confederates had acquired the "Bordeaux ram" the same day she sailed from France. He immediately relayed the news to Seward, adding that fifty sailors shipped from London, probably to join the ironclad, and suggested the secretary alert American coastal towns and ports of her possible arrival. Dudley also contacted U.S. consuls asking them to let him know if they spotted the vessel. Within two weeks he could report the *Stonewall* (he now knew her name) had entered a Spanish port for repairs and that she had received her armament, crew, and supplies from the English steamer *City of Richmond.*

Dudley also wrote "Mr. Draper," the Collector of New York, warning him that the ironclad might "attempt to run into some of the northern sea port towns and lay them in ashes," possibly gaining entrance by flying the English flag "as has been frequently done by these piratical vessels."[40]

The *Stonewall*, indeed, had entered a Spanish port. She sprang a leak her first day out and "limped" into La Coruna. Crewmen recalled "her decks and turrets were flooded, and since both leak, her quarters, both for men and officers, were wholly unfit to be occupied."[41] In addition to the leak, her sails were inadequate, she could carry only enough coal for five days' steaming, and her guns would be ineffective in any but calm seas. The *Stonewall*'s repairs were so extensive, Page moved her across the bay to El Ferrol's larger facility. The captain eventually traveled to Paris and met with Slidell and Barron to discuss a course of action. Bulloch sent Captain Tessier and an experienced engineer to El Ferrol to direct repairs. The *Stonewall* was not ready to continue her voyage until March 24, 1865.[42]

Federal authorities used these weeks to try and convince French and Spanish authorities to seize the *Stonewall* or at least refuse her repairs. Bigelow, who became acting minister after Dayton's death in December, meanwhile ordered Captain Thomas Craven, of the U.S.S. *Niagara*, to El Ferrol. The *Niagara* arrived on February 14, and the U.S.S. *Sacramento* joined her a few days later. Bulloch wrote that the *Niagara* was a "large, powerful frigate, mounting ten 150-pounder Parrot rifled guns[,] . . . a ship of great speed, and could easily have kept clear of the *Stonewall*'s dangerous beak," and that the *Sacramento* was "a corvette, very heavily armed for her class." On March 24, the *Stonewall* stowed her upper masts, hoisted her flag, and prepared for battle. A Spanish frigate escorted her out into international waters. To the Confederate crew's amazement, neither the *Niagara* nor the *Sacramento* moved to stop the ironclad. Page wrote Bulloch, "This will doubtless seem as inexplicable to you as it is to me, and to all of us. To suppose that those two heavily armed men-of-war were *afraid* of the *Stonewall* is to me incredible, yet the fact of their conduct was such as I have stated to you."[43] The U.S. Navy twice court-martialed Captain Craven for not trying to stop the ship.

Failing to convict him, the navy ultimately allowed him to serve until his retirement. He had apparently believed Dudley and the others when they described the ironclads as unstoppable.[44]

While negotiating for the *Stonewall*, Bulloch also searched for a suitable replacement for the *Alabama*, lost in June 1864. Knowing Dudley closely watched his comings and goings and that further efforts to build a warship in England would be futile, in September 1864 Bulloch sent an experienced ship's broker to scour Scotland's ports for a suitable cruiser to convert into a commerce raider. The broker telegraphed Bulloch that the *Sea King*, well suited for his purposes, was available. Bulloch knew the ship. He and Lieutenant Robert R. Carter, while in Glasgow the previous year, had admired her; but she had already loaded for Bombay, India, and was not for sale. Bulloch, however, "took careful note" that she would return in eight to ten months. He immediately telegraphed the broker to buy the ship, after careful inspection. Bulloch later explained that if he himself had inspected the ship or had been near her it would "be the immediate occasion of a consular report to Mr. Adams," who would promptly notify Lord Russell and "the hope of getting the ship to sea as a Confederate cruiser would be nipped in the bud."[45]

Bulloch had good reason for caution. Dudley, too, had spotted the *Sea King* in 1863 and suspected she was a Confederate cruiser. When she loaded and sailed for Bombay, he returned his attention to stopping the Laird ironclads, but the ship could hardly have been better suited for commerce raiding if Bulloch had ordered her for that purpose. A 200-foot long "composite" ship of 1,126 tons, she had iron frames and beams covered with East Indian teak. Her 800-horsepower engine could drive her along at eleven knots or she could retract her screw propeller and operate under sail. With the screw retracted, she logged 330 miles in 25 hours under sail alone on her voyage to India. Built as a troop transport, she had ample quarters for a commerce raider's officers and men. Writing to Navy Secretary Mallory, Bulloch noted "this was perhaps the only ship of her type and class in Great Britain."[46]

Following Maury's example, neither Bulloch nor anyone "having the faintest odour of 'rebellion'" went near the ship. Instead, Bulloch asked Richard Wright, Charles Prioleau's father-in-law and a British citizen, to be his agent. On October 7, 1864, Wright bought the *Sea King* in his own name for £45,000 sterling (about $219,600), ballasted her with coal, and cleared her for India. Bulloch selected Captain Peter S. Corbett to get the *Sea King* to sea, and Wright gave Corbett power of attorney to sell the ship at any time after leaving London. Lieutenant Carter had returned, meanwhile, from the South, and Bulloch sent him to Glasgow to accompany Captain Corbett to a rendezvous point and assess alterations the ship would need for conversion to a raider.[47]

Bulloch also needed a ship to meet the *Sea King* with supplies, armament, and crew. Again he employed a broker, who suggested he examine a new iron steamer "built for . . . the packet service between Liverpool and Ireland." After taking a short passage on her and seeing that she fit his needs, Bulloch purchased the *Laurel* and turned her over to a Liverpool shipping agent. As a ruse, the agent advertised for freight and passengers going to Havana, Cuba, but in reality the freight would be "stores and armament for the cruiser, and the passengers were the officers and a few choice men for her."[48] By October 5, 1864, both vessels were ready. Bulloch directed the *Sea King*, which was now in London ostensibly for additional cargo, to sail as early as possible on October 8. When the *Sea King* telegraphed that she was safely away, the *Laurel* with her freight already loaded boarded her passengers, including Lieutenant Commanding James I. Waddell, that same evening and proceeded at once to sea. The two ships rendezvoused at Las Desertas, an uninhabited island near Madeira, Azores, where they quickly transferred the arms and supplies to the *Sea King* and Captain Corbett "sold" her to Lieutenant Waddell, her new captain. Waddell then commissioned her the C.S.S. *Shenandoah*.[49]

Dudley did not learn the *Sea King* had sailed for another week. On October 15, Moran wrote Dudley detailing her sale to Wright and Wright's giving power of attorney to Corbett. Moran did not recognize Wright's name, but Dudley did. He realized immediately that the Confederates had a new cruiser. Three days later, the consul furnished Secretary Seward details of the transaction, including sale price, buyer, captain, number of crew, and particulars about the *Laurel*. The one bit of information he had wrong, he wrote that Captain Semmes would be her captain. He cautioned, "If I mistake not she will prove herself a dangerous craft to our commerce." Dudley's details were quite accurate but too late: the *Sea King* had already arrived at Las Desertas.[50]

Bulloch gave Waddell very general instructions for his cruise. He did, however, stipulate that he had promised the *Sea King*'s "ostensible owner," Wright, that after commissioning the *Shenandoah* should take no prizes for thirty days. This would give Captain Corbett enough time to return to England and remove Wright's name from the ship's registration. Bulloch also explained that Waddell should visit Northern whaling grounds in the Pacific and Arctic oceans and destroy the whaling fleets there. Waddell did not heed the first instruction, and the *Shenandoah* captured her initial prize on October 30, 1864, less than two weeks after commissioning. She proceeded toward the Pacific around the Cape of Good Hope, capturing and burning a few other ships before stopping in Melbourne, Australia, on January 25, 1865. Dudley had already alerted William Blanchard, the local American consul, that the *Shenandoah* might be coming his way. Despite Blanchard's protests, local officials not only allowed the ship to stay until March 18 but received her with jubilation. Waddell even managed surreptitiously to fill out his crew, much to Blanchard's chagrin.[51]

The *Shenandoah* then headed for the South Pacific, where she sank four whalers on April 1, 1865, in the harbor of Ascension in the Carolinas. Although in late May Waddell read in a captured newspaper that Lee had surrendered, he chose not to believe the newspaper and sailed on. After reaching the Bering Sea, he quickly sank so many whalers he had to tow a string of whaleboats behind the *Shenandoah* to carry all the prisoners. On a single day, June 28, he captured twelve whalers and burned nine. Not until August 1865 did Waddell encounter an English ship and definitely learn the war was over. He spiked his guns and headed back to Liverpool. In ten months the *Shenandoah* had captured thirty-eight ships, burning thirty-two valued at $1,361,983.[52]

As with the other ships, Dudley continued gathering evidence long after the *Sea King* had sailed. In November 1864, when the *Calibar* returned carrying crewmen from the *Laurel* and the *Sea King* who had refused to sail on a Confederate commerce raider, Dudley gathered affidavits describing the *Sea King*'s voyage to the Azores and the equipment and crew transfer from the *Laurel*. He quickly wrote Seward with more details. At Dudley's instigation, Adams pressed Lord Russell to prosecute Corbett. A British court eventually found Corbett not guilty of violating the Foreign Enlistment Act. Although Dudley had not prevented the *Shenandoah* from sailing, he would soon hold her fate in his hands. The war would soon be over and his "day of reckoning" was at hand.[53]

THE DAYS
OF RECKONING

7

Americans in Liverpool had only three days to revel in the "glorious news" that the war had ended before word came of the "calamity which has befallen the country," President Lincoln's assassination. Crowds gathered in Liverpool and all of England to "express indignation and abhorrence at the brutal and fiendish murder" of the president. Liverpool's public buildings and British ships flew their flags at half staff for three days honoring Lincoln's memory. Dudley draped the consulate in black and wore a black armband for six months.[1]

Neither the Union victory nor Lincoln's death ended Dudley's struggles against the Confederacy and its allies. Seward continued as secretary of state under President Andrew Johnson, and Dudley maintained his position as consul. Dudley, as a lawyer, would continue building the case he had started in 1862 to prove Great Britain's negligence in the commerce raiders' construction and escape. Now, at last, the American lawyer would have his day in court and he served his client, the American people, well.

Liverpool as the center for Confederate shipbuilding and the home office of that government's European "banker" Fraser, Trenholm and Company was the key to unraveling Southern finances abroad. Dudley would spend the next seven years recovering millions of dollars of Confederate property that now belonged to the U.S. government as spoils of war. He and many other Northerners also wanted retribution for what they perceived as the British government's responsibility for losses inflicted by the C.S.S. *Alabama* and her sister ships. Taking custody of the remaining Confederate ships was his first priority, however.

Dudley did not have to worry about the ironclad C.S.S. *Stonewall*. After she sailed, untouched, past the U.S.S. *Niagara* and the U.S.S. *Sacramento,* the *Stonewall* stopped in Portugal to recoal before heading for Nassau and then on to Havana, Cuba. In Havana, Captain Thomas J. Page learned that General Robert E. Lee had surrendered and Union troops had captured Jefferson Davis. On May 19, 1865, realizing the war was over Page surrendered his ship to the Cuban captain general, who gave Page $16,000 to pay off his crew. In July Cuba delivered the ironclad to the United States, who subsequently sold her to Japan. American admiral S. W. Godon later inspected the *Stonewall* and expressed the belief that Northern warships could have defeated her. "The *Canonicus* would have crushed her" and "the *Monadnock* could have taken her beyond doubt."[2]

With the ironclad accounted for, Dudley addressed the other, lesser-known, Southern vessels. Before Commodore Barron left Europe, he transferred the C.S.S. *Rappahannock* to Bulloch's control on February 28, 1865. Bulloch, already aware that the ship's limitations did not warrant spending dwindling funds to repair her, completed a "nominal sale" to a ship's broker, who sailed her to Liverpool as an English ship. When she arrived on July 8, Dudley immediately brought suit against her, as well as the C.S.S. *Sumter* and the C.S.S. *Tallahassee*. British courts ceded the latter two to the United States in June 1866. Dudley sold the *Sumter* for £1,140 sterling (approximately $5,563) and the *Tallahassee* for £4,600 (approximately $22,448), which he deposited in the U.S. account with Baring Brothers. Suits and counter suits snarled the *Rappahannock* in the courts until February 1867, when

Dudley took possession and then sold her for £5,200 (approximately $25,376). The C.S.S. *Alexandra,* too, became embroiled in the courts after the United States seized her and Prioleau claimed she was his private property and not subject to confiscation.[3]

All the ships were now accounted for, except the C.S.S. *Shenandoah.* And where was she? After learning of the *Sea King's* sale to the Confederates and her subsequent conversion to the commerce raider *Shenandoah* in November, Dudley followed the news of her voyage around the world as well as he could with the limited communications of the time. He alerted American consuls to be on the lookout for her, and William Blanchard, the consul at Melbourne, Australia, reported back that she had sailed from that port on March 18, 1865. She sank four whalers in the Carolinas in the South Pacific on April 1 and then disappeared. U.S. warships combed the Pacific Ocean with no results. Dudley could only speculate as to her location, but rumor placed her in Manila in May. Her destruction of America's whaling fleet in the Bering Sea remained a mystery to the world for several weeks. On May 1 Confederate agents in England ordered the *Shenandoah* to cease operations and return to England as soon as possible. Of course the orders did not reach Captain James Waddell, so he continued burning Union whalers until ice threatened to imprison his ship. With few prospective victims remaining, he sailed south. Off California's Baja Coast on August 2, he received news of the war's end from the British bark *Barracouta.* Americans, including Dudley, learned of the sighting, but despite the American fleet's best efforts, the *Shenandoah* disappeared again.[4]

With still no word on the *Shenandoah's* whereabouts, Dudley sailed for the United States and a ninety-day leave of absence on September 6, to "recruit" his health and tend to pressing business. After only a month in New Jersey, he returned to Liverpool, arriving on November 8, and missed the *Shenandoah's* dramatic entrance into her home port by two days. As she approached Liverpool on November 6, a pilot came aboard and confirmed "the war has been over so long people have got through talking about it."[5] As she neared the harbor, a telltale scraping sound signaled that the ship had run aground and stuck fast on a bar. Fortunately, the morning tide floated her free and she sailed through a thick fog into the Mersey River. After Captain Waddell maneuvered his ship alongside the H.M.S. *Donegal,* an officer from that ship came aboard and officially notified the *Shenandoah*'s captain that the war was over. At 10 a.m. Waddell, in full dress uniform, called his crew together and thanked them for their service. The quartermaster then lowered the Confederate flag, ending the commerce raider's final cruise.[6]

With the United States clamoring for retribution for losses inflicted by the commerce raiders, the reappearance of a notorious perpetrator emphasized England's role in the devastating ventures of *Shenandoah* and her sister ships. The next day's *London Times* best reflected British attitude toward the ship's return to Liverpool: "The reappearance of the *Shenandoah* in British waters at the present juncture is an untoward and unwelcome event." The *Pall Mall Gazette* remarked, "Small thanks are due to the commander of the *Shenandoah* for the preference which he has given to Liverpool for the purpose of bringing his cruising to an end." In a letter to Foreign Secretary Russell, Waddell explained his reason for choosing Liverpool. Upon learning of the Confederacy's collapse, he believed he no longer had authority to command the vessel or to destroy her as she was now U.S. property. He, therefore, considered Liverpool the suitable port to surrender his ship to the British government, "for such disposal as in its wisdom should be deemed proper."[7]

Russell, fully aware that Minister Adams stood ready to present American claims for reimbursement for damage wrought by the British-built raiders, turned Waddell's letter over to the Crown's law officers. After deliberating for forty-eight hours, they responded that the *Shenandoah,* as a legally commissioned Confederate warship, had the right to raid Union merchant ships. She was, however, now U.S. government property and should be turned over to American authorities. The Crown's legal advisers also stated that any British crew members should be tried under the Foreign Enlistment Act, all others were to be released. Captain J. G. Paynter of the *Donegal* immediately informed Waddell that the crew members who were still on board, except British subjects, were free to go. When Waddell asked,

"We are released unconditionally?" Paynter replied, "Without conditions." Not surprisingly, none of the crewmen acknowledged British citizenship, claiming—sometimes in thick English accents or Scottish brogues—to have been born in Virginia, Tennessee, or Texas. The next day Waddell, using money Bulloch had reserved for the purpose, gave each officer between £50 and £100 sterling, and the quartermaster paid the crew about one shilling for every three they were due. On November 11 the British government turned the *Shenandoah* over to Dudley.[8]

Unlike almost everyone else, Dudley seemed happy to see the *Shenandoah* in Liverpool. He immediately telegraphed Minister Adams, who directed him to accept the ship and await further instructions. Dudley wanted to send the ship to New York, but Adams was content to wait and do nothing "to help Britain out of the mess it has got itself into." He felt the United States would "lose nothing by the passage of time; Great Britain does." Adams did not share his reasoning with Dudley but simply replied that he was "not prepared to give a decided answer." Dudley, meanwhile, selected Captain Thomas Freeman, an American working for the British shipping firm Guion and Company, to take charge and clean the vessel and her engines. Freeman had already inspected the ship and reported "abominable filth" everywhere. He asked for extra men and "a hundred pounds of chloride and lime and one dozen brooms. The sight of things on board this ship is enough to make a person sick." The ship's condition lends support to rumors of near mutiny over Waddell's decision to sail back to Liverpool.[9]

A week later, Adams relented and authorized Dudley to appoint a captain and send the *Shenandoah* to New York. Dudley "lost no time" naming Freeman captain and hiring a crew, including a British engineer and staff to maintain the ship's engines. On November 21, barely two weeks after she reached Liverpool, Dudley dispatched the ship to New York. She was clean, in good condition, coaled, and provisioned for the voyage. Captain Freeman, "an experienced commander in whom [Dudley had] confidence" and fifty-five men and officers set sail. Dudley considered the *Shenandoah* to be "a very fine vessel" and reported he had done everything "to ensure a quick and secure passage across the Atlantic."[10]

Unfortunately the ship encountered a North Atlantic winter gale, which tore through her sails and forced her back to Liverpool. Captain Freeman reported the *Shenandoah* lacked the steam power to make headway through the gale and her sails were not strong enough to withstand the storm's pressure. The ship's hull, mast, and rigging, however, remained in good condition. Although disappointed, Dudley ordered new sails, additional coal, and provisions and prepared to send her back out within a week. Freeman soon reported the new sails were on board along with additional coal and provisions; however, he would be unable to command her as his company now required his services. The crew also refused to attempt a second voyage.[11]

To his chagrin, Dudley learned in a "Strictly Confidential" letter from Benjamin Moran of the American legation in London that Minister Adams apparently "meant from the first to throw the responsibility of sending her home on *you*. I think he secretly chuckles over Freeman's unfortunate return." Dudley, meanwhile, sought to reassure Secretary of State Seward that he had done everything possible "that human foresight could suggest with the limited knowledge [he] had, to guard against accident and to secure success." The consul next telegraphed Rear Admiral Louis M. Goldsborough, commander of the U.S. Navy's European squadron, asking for "a competent commander and two or more officers" to take the ship to New York. Possibly resenting orders from a civilian consul or perhaps simply not wanting to get involved, Goldsborough declined, in a telegram stating he was "not satisfied that the government at home relished the acceptance of the Shenandoah."[12]

Frustrated in his attempt to send the *Shenandoah* to New York, Dudley stowed the sails and secured the ship's property, had expert crewmen from the *Donegal* remove and store the powder and live shells, and then placed her in the Birkenhead docks while awaiting Seward's instructions. In March 1866, Seward directed Dudley to sell the *Shenandoah* at public auction, but to ensure that a belligerent nation did not buy her. After getting expert appraisals ranging from £10,000 to £14,500 sterling, Dudley sold her to a Liverpool merchant for £15,750 (approximately $75,700). The purchaser signed a certificate that the ship would not be used for warlike purposes. The ship's stores sold for nearly $7,000. Dudley kept the *Shenandoah*'s stationery for office use and her barometer to hang outside the consulate "for use of the seamen transacting business" there. He also asked for a 1 percent commission to cover his expenses and extra trouble and work, but Seward denied the request.[13]

Tangible Confederate assets, especially ships, were easy to locate and, if they had engaged in commerce raiding, readily confiscated as U.S. government property. Smaller items and liquid assets, including money, proved more difficult to find and establish ownership. With the war's end, the federal government gained access to Confederate records at Richmond, which helped clarify contracts emanating from North America, but European transactions remained obscure. The State and Treasury departments engaged agents to find hidden Confederate property and funds in England and France in return for a percentage of the assets recovered. Dudley spent many hours following up on information often based on rumors. Then, when the leads proved fruitful, he passed weeks, months, and years in English courts trying to gain possession. He initially operated under the State Department–imposed restriction that he could not acknowledge the rebelling states had established a de facto government. Seward and the administration still condemned Great Britain for what they perceived as hasty recognition of Confederate belligerent rights and planned, at some future time, to make this a claims issue. If the rebelling states had not created a de facto government, then all contracts signed by their agents were illegal and the United States could claim all Confederate property without having to satisfy liens against it. This would also strengthen the U.S. case against England. The English courts soon ruled that the Confederacy was a de facto government and American suits would be considered only on that basis.[14]

Although the federal government appointed Caleb Cushing to oversee the lawsuits in the British courts, Cushing opted to stay in the United States "until after the completion of all the preliminary investigation of the facts here in several cases." Apparently the "preliminary" investigation never concluded, since Cushing remained in the United States. In August 1866, Secretary

Seward, writing on behalf of both State and Treasury departments, authorized Dudley to recover "any public property formerly belonging to the late so called Confederate Government . . . within the limits of your Consulate," by legal proceedings if necessary. The Treasury Department would pay legal expenses.[15]

Dudley learned that the *Aline* had sailed from Havana for Liverpool carrying fourteen hundred bales of cotton belonging to the Confederate government and valued at $160,000. When the *Aline* reached port, Dudley immediately claimed the cotton as U.S. property. Fraser, Trenholm and Company brought suit, stating the company had spent £20,000 sterling (approximately $97,400) on the shipment, in addition to other money due from the Confederate government. Dudley counter sued but asked Seward to send proof of Confederate government ownership.[16]

Dudley quickly discovered how frustrating English courts could be for an American lawyer. He considered British law to be "a cunningly devised system to extort money from the people for the benefit of the profession." He explained to Seward that every step in a proceeding required an expert legal opinion. To obtain the Crown's attorney general's ruling Dudley hired solicitors in Liverpool, who in turn had to employ other solicitors in London. The attorney general, however, refused to render an opinion without a junior barrister employed to assist him. Then another barrister was needed as the deciding vote in case the attorney general and his junior barrister deadlocked. To Dudley, an American lawyer experienced in "our straight forward way of doing business," the English legal system was designed to bleed and swindle the clients.[17]

To further complicate matters, Dudley found "as much bitterness against the United States among the judges and in the courts as there was at any time during the rebellion." Proceedings in the "Cotton Case" seemed to confirm his assertion. The court first ruled that, since the cotton had shipped through Texas, that state's governor or his representative should appear. Dudley finally, after repeated requests, succeeded in obtaining a letter from the governor appointing the consul as his agent. Next the court allowed Fraser, Trenholm and Company lawyers to name President Andrew Johnson as a party in their counter suit and demanded that he appear personally to receive notice. Eventually the court allowed Dudley's attorneys to accept the notification. Final resolution for the case languished until it later became part of an 1871 settlement between the United States and Charles Prioleau.[18]

Dudley filed another suit against Fraser, Trenholm and Company to force the firm to open its books and account for the Confederate funds or equipment still within its control. As the Southern government's European financial agents, this company's records would disclose most of the Confederate contracts with British firms and greatly assist in Dudley's legal proceedings to recover Confederate property. He also sued Charles Prioleau for possession of the *Alexandra,* which had converted to the merchant ship *Mary.*[19]

Proceeding with the various suits as the State and Treasury departments had directed, Dudley was shocked in November 1866 when his solicitor informed him that all the litigation between the United States and Charles Prioleau had been settled effective that same morning. Unbeknownst to Dudley, London consul Freeman Morse and Paris consul Montgomery Gibbs had traveled to Liverpool and negotiated a clandestine deal with Prioleau. Dudley immediately wrote Seward asking for an explanation and remarking that if "duty did not require them to consult with me who had charge of the cases" and the person who knew more about Fraser, Trenholm and Company's dealings with the Confederacy than anyone else, "at least common courtesy would seem to dictate that the first notice or intimation that the deed had been accomplished should not come from our opponents." Dudley also indicated that both Morse and Gibbs knew he would be away from Liverpool for one or two days and they could have easily arranged to meet with him if they had so desired. Although he had not seen details of the settlement, it apparently allowed the "firm that have been the most active in aiding the rebellion and fitting our piratical expeditions" to retain £150,000 "or over seven hundred thousand dollars when there [was] no necessity to do so."[20]

Dudley included copies of letters he had just received from Morse and Gibbs explaining their actions. Morse claimed that

he received a request to meet with Prioleau to discuss a settlement, and "holding power both from the State and Treasury Departments to 'compromise & settle' just such cases," he felt
compelled to agree. Dudley's absence had precluded Morse's including him as he would have preferred. When Morse proposed
shifting the negotiations to Dudley, Prioleau refused. After six
hours of negotiations, they agreed that Prioleau would give the
United States free access to the company books and a sworn
statement of all Confederate property held or contracted by Fraser,
Trenholm and Company, and the company would receive three-
fifths of "all just and legal liens they have on the property." The
United States would also withdraw all suits against the company
in the British courts and a suit in the United States to recover the
Wren, a company-owned blockade runner. Morse concluded, "By
this arrangement we reach far better results than can possibly be
reached by long expensive, irritating & doubtful law suits in the
courts of this country where all the leanings are against us."
Gibbs's much shorter note to Dudley commented, "I know that in
the interest of the government you will rejoice that every point
which could have been gained by the favorable result of these te-
dious and expensive law suits has been reached by this most judicious arrangement."[21]

Far from rejoicing, Dudley took exception not only to the
way Morse and Gibbs had disrespected him but with the settlement itself. He had acquired a copy of the agreement from Minister Adams's office in London. In response to Morse's letter,
Dudley pointed out differences between Morse's version to Dudley and the agreement itself. There was no provision in the settlement for Fraser, Trenholm and Company to provide a sworn
statement of all Confederate property held or controlled by
them. Also, contrary to Morse's account that the company
would receive three-fifths of just and legal liens, the agreement
stated "the claim Fraser, Trenholm & Co against the late Confederate government is agreed at £150,000 [approximately
$730,000] and that this is to be first paid and if any surplus re-
mains it is to go to the United States." Lest there be any doubt
about his feelings, Dudley informed Morse, "I regard this agreement or settlement as most unjust and unfair to the govern-

ment and the conduct of yourself and Mr Gibbs in entering into it under the circumstances and in the manner it was done as most discourteous and disrespectful to myself."[22] Dudley soon learned from Minister Adams that the State Department disavowed the Morse-Gibbs negotiated settlement.

Dudley later discovered that Morse had instituted a suit in London to recover property and money from "Major Furgerson a rebel agent and quartermaster," who had come to England to buy clothing and munitions, and General Colin McRae, the Confederate agent sent to administer proceeds from the $15 million Erlanger loan. Morse based his suit on information supplied by "Mr Fisher an American lawyer residing in London." In return for Fisher's help, Morse agreed to pay him 25 percent of all Confederate assets recovered. After Fisher paid his expenses, he and Morse were to split the remainder of the 25 percent. Fisher also told Dudley that, after the government repudiated the agreement Morse and Gibbs had reached with Fraser, Trenholm and Company, Morse declined to accept anything from the Furgerson case. Fisher had already told Minister Adams and Benjamin Moran of the arrangement, and Dudley informed Secretary Seward and included copies of Fisher's letters. Apparently feeling Morse had acted dishonestly, Seward then transferred the Furgerson and McRae suits to Dudley's control. It must have been especially galling to Dudley three years later when, in 1869, Hamilton Fish, the new state secretary in the Grant administration, named Morse consul general for Great Britain, and in theory Dudley's superior.[23]

In May 1867, shortly after Seward negated the Morse-Gibbs deal with Fraser, Trenholm and Company, that company stopped paying its debts and then filed for bankruptcy. Caleb Cushing and the company's American partners signed an agreement to account for all Confederate assets, including nine ships, within the company's control. The United States also would receive proceeds from the contested cotton for which Dudley had sued, plus court costs. Theodore Wagner, the acting partner in the United States, telegraphed Prioleau to "abstain from all aggressive action," as further legal proceeding would only add to company expenses. Wagner promised to soon leave for England

and ensure "speedy conclusion." The United States in return did not concede any balance of money due to Fraser, Trenholm and Company. Cushing, apparently feeling quite satisfied, concluded to Dudley, "Thus you see that in this point alone we trump the cards of Morse and Gibbs."[24]

When Prioleau learned his partners had settled, however, he denied that the American agreement affected him, a naturalized British citizen living and doing business in England. He informed his solicitors that "he was not going to submit to its terms, but would fight [the United States] to the last."[25] The Fraser, Trenholm and Company partnership officially dissolved in March 1868. Wagner finally reached Liverpool in July 1868 and turned over the company's accounts concerning the cotton aboard the *Aline*, but Prioleau counter sued, and both the cotton cases and the suit asking for full accounting of Fraser, Trenholm and Company's Confederate dealings in Great Britain dragged on. As Secretary Seward prepared to leave office in early 1869 with the Johnson administration, Dudley summarized the status of the cases against Prioleau and his ex-partners. At war's end they had in their possession nine steamships, which cost the "so called Confederate government" over £54,413 sterling (approximately $265,000), $100,000 in gold, $1 million in cotton, and untold millions had passed through their hands and remained unaccounted for. The *Mary*, known earlier as the *Alexandra*, remained in the London docks for final court determination of ownership. Negotiations to resolve the cases were ongoing in Washington and Dudley's instructions were to await the outcome.[26]

With the inauguration of President Ulysses Grant in March 1869, Hamilton Fish became secretary of state and E. R. Hoar the attorney general. Hoar recommended and Fish agreed to discontinuing several of the suits pending in England, including the one against McRae and Blakeley Ordnance, the company that made large guns for Confederate commerce raiders and coastal defense. Dudley had earlier resolved the Furgerson case. The suits against Prioleau and the British office of Fraser, Trenholm and Company were to continue, however. Dudley asked that the department reconsider the Blakeley case believing he could soon resolve it. Blakeley himself had died, and liquidators now held the property (originally costing £22,980 or approximately $112,000) and seemed eager to conclude proceedings. Secretary Fish agreed and ordered Dudley to take charge of the property when the courts released it, and the navy would send a ship to retrieve it. Finally, in mid-June 1871, the U.S.S. *Worcester* sailed from Liverpool with the Blakeley guns and shells and other equipment recovered from Fawcett, Preston and Company, builder of the *Alabama*'s engines.[27]

The courts did release the *Alexandra*, to be sold for £910 sterling (approximately $4,432) in 1869 with the money held in trust until final resolution. When Dudley returned to the United States in 1871 to once again rest and treat his ailing bowels, he took the opportunity to visit with Caleb Cushing in Washington. Cushing revealed he had reached an agreement with Prioleau that would include full accounting and resolve all outstanding issues. Dudley was to do no more with the suits until he received official instructions. In September 1872, however, the Prioleau and Fraser, Trenholm and Company suits remained active in court. Although it is difficult to accurately estimate the total amount Dudley recovered directly and helped recover indirectly, the sum must have run into the millions. But, perhaps his greatest contribution would be the evidence he amassed to support the U.S. "*Alabama* Claims."[28]

Dudley's health remained an issue throughout his tenure as consul in Liverpool. By mid-1871 he needed yet another leave. This time, however, he felt it was probably time to resign. "The strain has been very great upon me, so much so as to affect my health, and I fear continuance in office, with the like strain, will seriously undermine my constitution." Liverpool had also adversely affected the health of his daughter. He, therefore, notified the State Department that he intended to resign that autumn, and in anticipation, he had begun shipping his household goods back to Camden. Although he and his family traveled in Europe during the summer, by October the Dudleys were at home in New Jersey.[29]

Dudley assured the department he wanted to "contribute all in [his] power to secure success" before the upcoming tribunal set to meet in Geneva, Switzerland, to settle the U.S. grievances against Great Britain. Talks were to begin in December 1871 after the United States and Great Britain signed the Treaty of Washington earlier in the year agreeing to resolve the claims through arbitration. This treaty followed the U.S. Senate rejection in 1869 of a similar agreement, by the overwhelming vote of 54 to 1. Senator Charles Sumner, in arguing against that treaty, called for England to pay approximately $2 billion in "indirect claims" for extending the Civil War by recognizing Southern belligerent status and supplying the Confederate military. Although indirect claims had no precedent in international law, the American public quickly accepted Sumner's figures as the basis for any settlement. President Grant, eager for reelection in 1872, and other politicians hesitated to deny America's claim to this huge sum. Meanwhile British officials, led by Lord Russell after Palmerston's death in 1865, denied any liability and dismissed the indirect claims as preposterous. By late 1871, however, William Gladstone was prime minister, and after years of hostile posturing on both sides a settlement seemed possible. The Prussian Army's occupation of Paris following the defeat of Emperor Napoléon III's French forces gave Great Britain additional incentive to resolve any differences with the United States. The Washington Treaty, therefore, included one protocol that made it much more palatable to all Americans, including Dudley—the British government's regret "for the escape, under whatever circumstances, of the *Alabama* and other vessels from British ports, and for the depredations committed by those vessels." The American public would probably not have accepted the treaty nor would the Senate have approved it without this nominal apology. Both sides were now ready to decide the outstanding claims issues.[30]

In his letter of resignation, Dudley left the possibility open for further official service by offering to transfer to the healthier climate of Berne, Switzerland, or Brussels, Belgium. Robert Schenck, the new minister in London, and others then impressed upon Dudley his importance to the American claims case. He agreed to resume his consul duties, noting, "I can assure you I am most anxious to do and contribute all in my power to secure our success before this Tribunal and I think I can be of some service to the government in bringing about this result."[31] He returned to Liverpool in November 1871 and immediately "commenced to collect additional evidence to be laid before the Tribunal to meet at Geneva to settle the Alabama case."[32]

In anticipation of this opportunity, Dudley had amassed "voluminous correspondence and files . . . from the commencement of the rebellion" supporting his contention that Great Britain had not fulfilled its obligations as a neutral nation. He hoped to prove she had been negligent in allowing warships, built to make war on a friendly nation, to be constructed and manned in her ports. Long after the *Florida, Alabama, Shenandoah,* and others had sailed, Dudley continued seeking witnesses against them and taking affidavits. Like a good district attorney, he spent years building a case that he believed he would someday help prosecute. Even before leaving for his intended resignation, he forwarded several affidavits, letters, and depositions to Minister Schenck. Dudley also contacted everyone he knew had served aboard one of the commerce raiders and retained several to be available to give affidavits detailing their service on these vessels.[33]

The State Department, meanwhile, asked Dudley to review the case that Assistant State Secretary Bancroft Davis and Yale President Theodore D. Woolsey had prepared for America. After reading the text Dudley asked the department to delete the phrase "the great mass of the industrial classes were understood to sympathize with them" ("them" referring to the United States). He explained that although Goldwin Smith, Tom Hughes, and other Englishmen asserted this to be true, Dudley had moved among the British, and "I tell you that nine tenths of the people of England including the working class as well as the other classes were against us and sympathized with the South. I tested it in many ways by the newspapers they read, their children in schools, the public meetings they attended and by mingling and talking with the working class."

Dudley reiterated his contention to Assistant State Secretary Davis, adding that Minister Schenck mistakenly believed there were British citizens who would willingly give evidence or swear to depositions supporting the Northern court cases. "They do not love us now any better than they did during the war. . . . Now as then no one is willing to aid us without being paid and well paid. . . . I knew of fifty men who were concerned in these transactions but not one of them will volunteer to give evidence."[34]

James Bulloch, who remained in England after the war, agreed. His personal observations and the opinions of other Confederate agents who lived in England during the war convinced him "that the great majority of the people in Great Britain—at least among the classes a traveller, or a man of business, or a frequenter of the clubs, would be likely to meet—were on the Southern side." Furthermore, he never met anyone from the British Army or Royal Navy "who did not warmly sympathize with the South. . . . The assertion so frequently made by the representatives of the United States to the foregoing effect was, therefore, in all probability true."[35]

Dudley continued building the case. He interviewed and obtained new affidavits from former commerce-raider crewmen. He acquired crew lists and logs from the raiders and the ships that had sailed to meet them with their armament, and information on blockade runners. Dudley found a Liverpool merchant willing to swear to Fraser, Trenholm and Company's financing of and Bulloch's overseeing construction of the *Alabama*. He journeyed to Paris, Italy, and Munich compiling more evidence and then on to Geneva to deliver the information and confer with American negotiators, including American representative to the tribunal and former minister to London, Charles Francis Adams.[36]

The Treaty of Washington called for a tribunal of five members, one each from Brazil, Great Britain, Italy, Switzerland, and the United States. The optimism with which the meeting began quickly faded when the U.S. demands included the "indirect claims" first proposed by Senator Sumner. Great Britain believed the treaty had already resolved this issue and refused to even discuss the matter. After a six-month impasse and on the brink of a complete breakdown in proceedings, Adams, "assuming a heavy responsibility . . . not as an arbitrator representing my country, but as representing all nations," secretly proposed the arbitrators "individually and collectively" conclude that international law did not support the indirect claims and "they, therefore, should be excluded from consideration." The others agreed, and on June 19 a unanimous vote to exclude the indirect claims broke the impasse. This opened the way to quickly resolving the remaining issues. On September 14, 1872, the tribunal by a four-to-one vote (Sir Alexander Cockburn, the British delegate, disagreed) awarded the United States $15 million for direct damages caused by the *Alabama,* the *Florida,* and the *Shenandoah* after she left Melbourne, Australia. Dudley's evidence undoubtedly contributed much to the tribunal's final decision.[37]

Neither the American nor the British public applauded the settlement. Americans expected $2 billion and the British anticipated paying nothing. British prime minister William Gladstone considered the settlement "harsh in its extent and unjust in its bases"; but by 1880 he reconsidered and lauded the example of two proud nations going "in peace and concord before a judicial tribunal" instead of resorting "to the arbitrament of the sword."[38] The eventual amity between the two nations did not come about immediately after settling the *Alabama* claims. Americans were slow to forgive Britain's sympathy for the South. There was also continued bickering over fishing rights, a proposed Central American canal, and a Venezuelan border dispute. But the settlement laid the groundwork for a cooperative and friendly alliance that has lasted for over 125 years and through two world wars.

Dudley must have felt a sense of satisfaction at his accomplishments as Liverpool's consul both during and after the war when he came to submit his resignation on October 7, 1872, but he could not have foreseen the long-term results of the Geneva agreement. In accepting his resignation, Secretary Fish affirmed the "fidelity, integrity and ability with which [Dudley] always discharged the important duties . . . during [his] long period of service."[39] Dudley returned to Camden, opened a law practice with his son, Edward, and played a minor role in Republican politics until his death on April 15, 1893.

That evening's *Camden Post* carried an appropriate and accurate eulogy for Thomas Haines Dudley, the man:

> Deeply religious in the Quaker sense, which makes each man alone responsible to his Maker and not to conventional ceremony, he was more spiritual minded than a practical prosaic lawyer and man of affairs would be taken to be, but never wore his heart upon his sleeve save to familiars. Hated by many through the prejudice and misconception engendered in political strife (as strong characters often are), misunderstood by many more because he would not stoop to conquer, he pursued the even tenor of his way in the respect and love of his confidants. Rarely heading public subscriptions, he was instant in good ways and works, and most of his generous benefactions were only known to the needy recipients.[40]

Camden and New Jersey had lost a leading citizen, Thomas Haines Dudley, a zealous Quaker who thwarted Confederate shipbuilding in England, a lawyer whose evidence gained the United States a fifteen million dollar claim settlement, and a diplomat whose contributions helped create an enduring peace with the country that had been our greatest rival.

NOTES

Prologue

1. Lincoln cited from Doris Kearns Goodwin, *Team of Rivals: The Political Genius of Abraham Lincoln* (New York: Simon and Schuster, 2005), 316; Seward cited from E. D. Adams, *Great Britain and the American Civil War* (New York: Russell and Russell, 1924), 1:124; Dean B. Mahin, *One War at a Time: The International Dimensions of the American Civil War* (Washington, DC: Brassey's, 1999), 7–8.

2. Lincoln cited from Goodwin, *Team of Rivals*, 711. For Seward, see Mahin, *One War at a Time*, 9; Howard Jones, *Union in Peril: The Crisis over British Intervention in the Civil War* (Chapel Hill: University of North Carolina Press, 1992), 7–8.

3. Rodman L. Underwood, *Stephen Russell Mallory: A Biography of the Confederate Navy Secretary and United States Senator* (Jefferson, NC: McFarland, 2005), 90–92, 169–70.

4. Declaration of Paris, quoted in Adams, *Great Britain*, 140.

1—The Making of a Consul

1. Sarah A. Wallace and Frances E. Gillespie, eds., *The Journal of Benjamin Moran, 1857–1865*, 2 vols. (Chicago: University of Chicago Press, 1949), 2:906–907; Douglas H. Maynard, "Thomas H. Dudley and Union Efforts to Thwart Confederate Activities in Great Britain" (Ph.D. diss., University of California, Los Angeles, June 1951), 12; William J. Potts, *Biographical Sketch of the late Hon. Thomas H. Dudley* (Philadelphia: Press of MacCall, 1895), 7.

2. Potts, *Dudley*, 3–6; "Thomas H. Dudley," *The Biographical Encyclopaedia of New Jersey of the Nineteenth Century* (Philadelphia: Galaxy, 1877), 300; Thomas Dudley, "Position on Capital Punishment," undated ms. in the Dudley Collection, Camden, Historical Society (hereafter listed as CNJHS).

3. Potts, *Dudley*, 5–7; John Needles to Dudley, 11, 13, 21 Oct. 1845, 25 Apr. 1846, Dudley to John Clement, 11 Jul. 1849, Caleb Green to Dudley, 19 Aug., Lemuel Davis to Dudley, Dec. 1853, in Dudley Collection, Huntington Library (hereafter listed as HL).

4. Dudley to Henry Carey, 28 Mar. 1856, in Edward Carey Gardiner Collection, Historical Society of Pennsylvania (hereafter listed as HSP).

5. Dudley to Carey, 28 Mar. 1856; T. Whitney to Dudley, 2 May, Carey to Dudley, 23 May, A. Q. Keasley to Dudley, 12 Sept. 1855, numerous bills for European hotels, Beach Vanderpool to Dudley, 19 May 1861 (HL); Dudley to F. W. Seward, 2 Dec. 1861 (CNJHS); T. P. Carpenter to Dudley, 5, 7 Sept. 1859 (HSP); Potts, *Dudley*, 7–8.

6. Charles McChesney, "Certificate of Appointment as Camden County Commissioner," 1 Apr. 1846, and W. A. Duer, "Certificate of Appointment as Alternate Whig Delegate," 24 May 1848 (CNJHS); Dudley to Carey, 11 Apr. 1855, 24 Nov. 1859 (HSP); Potts, *Dudley*, 8; Maynard, "Dudley," 1–2; McChesney to Dudley, 24 Aug. 1858 (HL).

7. Dudley to Carey, 24 Nov. 1859 (HSP).

8. Maynard, "Dudley," 4–9; Potts, *Dudley*, 9–11; David Davis to Dudley, 24, 29 Aug. 1860 (HL).

9. William Dayton to Dudley, 19 Mar., 23 Apr., James Sherman to Dudley, 21 Mar. 1861 (HL); James Tertius deKay, *The Rebel Raiders: The Astonishing History of the Confederacy's Secret Navy* (New York: Ballantine Books, 2002), 14–15.

10. Dayton to Dudley, 19 Mar., 23 Apr., Sherman to Dudley, 21 Mar. 1861 (HL).

11. Seward's appointee, DeWitt Littlejohn from New York, declined the appointment several weeks after being selected in April 1861. DeWitt Littlejohn to Seward, 27 Apr., 18, 10 Jun. 1861, Diplomatic Correspondence, Liverpool, National Archives (hereafter listed as DCLiv NA).

12. David Davis to Dudley, 12 Jul., Dudley to W. S. Seward, Nov. 1861 (HL); William Newell to Dudley, 29 Jul. 1880 (HSP); Maynard, "Dudley," 11–12; Seward, 15 Oct., Seward to C. F. Adams, 25 Oct. 1861 (Diplomatic Instructions of the Department of State, Great Britain, NA); Beverly Tucker to Secretary of State, 22 Feb. 1861 (DCLiv NA).

13. Ramsey Muir, *A History of Liverpool* (London, 1907), 192; Dudley, "Narrative," n.d. (HL); Maynard, "Dudley," 20–22.

14. Maynard, "Dudley," 22–31.

15. Ibid., 34–35.

16. Henry Adams, *A Cycle of Adams Letters, 1861–1865*, 2 vols. (Boston: Houghton Mifflin, 1920), 1:62; C. F. Adams to Seward, 17 May 1861 (Diplomatic Correspondence, Great Britain, NA); Dudley to Carey, 20 Oct. 1864 (HSP).

17. Dudley, "Narrative," n.d. (HL).

18. Dudley to William Chandler, 6 May 1868 (HL); Russell cited from Mahin, *One War at a Time*, 37.

19. F. W. Seward to Dudley, 28 Oct., Dudley to Zebina Eastman, Consul at Bristol, 12 Dec. 1861 (HL); Dudley, "Narrative," n.d. (HL).

20. John Bright to Dudley, 9 Dec. 1861 (HL); Dudley to Seward, 11 Dec. 1861 (DCLiv NA).

21. Norman B. Ferris, *The Trent Affair: A Diplomatic Crisis* (Knoxville: University of Tennessee Press, 1977), is an excellent account of the crisis and provides the details for this description.

22. Dudley to Seward, 29 Nov. 1861 (DCLiv NA).

23. Ivan Musicant, *Divided Waters: The Naval History of the Civil War* (New York: HarperCollins, 1995), 120.

24. Ibid.; Wallace and Gillespie, *Benjamin Moran,* 1:915; Dudley to Seward, 13 Dec. 1861 (DCLiv NA).

25. Musicant, *Divided Waters,* 122.

2—The *Florida*

1. Jim Dan Hill, *Sea Dogs of the Sixties: Farragut and Seven Contemporaries* (New York: A. S. Barnes, 1961), 65–66.

2. James D. Bulloch, *The Secret Service of the Confederate States in Europe,* 2 vols. (New York: Thomas Yoseloff, 1959), 1:22, 46, also 46–48.

3. William P. Roberts, "James Dunwoody Bulloch and the Confederate Navy," *North Carolina Historical Review* (July 1947): 315; Bulloch, *Secret Service,* 1:30.

4. Details for this paragraph and the following account are from Bulloch, *Secret Service,* 1:32–48.

5. DeKay, *Rebel Raiders,* 14.

6. Bulloch, *Secret Service,* 1:53–54.

7. Ibid., 1:65–67.

8. Frank Merli, *Great Britain and the Confederate Navy, 1861–1865* (Bloomington: Indiana University Press, 1970), 54–55; deKay, *Rebel Raisers,* 34–35; Wilding to Seward, 5 Jul., 14, 20, 28 Sept., 18 Oct. 1861 (DCLiv NA).

9. Bulloch, *Secret Service,* 1:51–68.

10. Ibid., 1:109–11; Wilding to William Seward, 14 Sept. 1861 (DCLiv NA).

11. Stanley Hoole, ed., *Confederate Foreign Agent: The European Diary of Major Edward C. Anderson* (Tuscaloosa, AL: Confederate Publishing, 1976), 70.

12. Bulloch, *Secret Service,* 1:112 (quote), 113–27.

13. Henry Wilding to Seward, 20 Sept., 18 Oct. 1861 (DCLiv NA).

14. Maynard, "Dudley," 57–63; Dudley to Seward, 11 Dec. 1861 (DCLiv NA).

15. Dudley to Seward, 24, 31 Jan. 1862 (DCLiv NA).

16. Ibid., 4 Feb. 1862.

17. Ibid., 12 Feb. 1862.

18. Ibid., 19, 21 Feb. 1862.

19. Maynard, "Dudley," 65–67.

20. William Parry to Wilding, 27 Feb. 1862 (HL).

21. Ibid., and 24 Feb. 1862 (HL); Dudley to Seward, 1 Mar. 1862 (DCLiv NA).

22. Dudley to Seward, 5, 7, 12 (quote) Mar. 1862 (DCLiv NA).

23. Warren Spencer, *The Confederate Navy in Europe* (Tuscaloosa: University of Alabama Press, 1983), 39–40.

24. Maynard, "Dudley," 72–73.

25. Dudley to Seward, 26, 27 Feb., 15 Mar. 1862 (DCLiv NA); Maynard, "Dudley," 73–74.

26. Bulloch, *Secret Service,* 1:152–53.

27. Ibid., 1:155–56.

28. Ibid., 1:157.

29. Ibid.; Dudley to Seward, 22, 26 Mar. 1862 (DCLiv NA).

30. Musicant, *Divided Waters,* 334.

31. Ibid., 334–35; Dudley to Seward, 15 Aug. 1862 (DCLiv NA).

32. Musicant, *Divided Waters,* 335–36.

33. Maynard, "Dudley," 74–75.

34. Musicant, *Divided Waters,* 340–41; Dudley to Seward, 22, 25, 26 Aug., 1, 9, 16 Sept. 1863 (DCLiv NA).

35. Musicant, *Divided Waters,* 341–42.

36. Dudley to Seward, 9 Nov. 1864 (DCLiv NA).

37. Frank Lawrence Owsley, Jr., *The C.S.S. Florida: Her Building and Operation* (Philadelphia: University of Pennsylvania Press, 1965), 161.

3—The *Alabama*

1. F. W. Seward to Dudley, 28 Oct., Dudley to Zebina Eastman, Consul at Bristol, 12 Dec. (quote) 1861 (HL).

2. Bulloch, *Secret Service,* 1:58–59.

3. Maynard, "Dudley," 93.

4. Bulloch, *Secret Service,* 1:62–63; Douglas H. Maynard, "Plotting the Escape of the *Alabama,*" *Journal of Southern History* 20 (1954): 199.

5. Wilding to Seward, 18 Oct. 1861 (DCLiv NA); Bulloch, *Secret Service,* 1:226–27.

6. Dudley to Seward, 11 Dec. 1861, 30 Jan., 4 Sept. 1862 (DCLiv NA); Maynard, "Dudley," 124.

7. Dudley to Seward, 1, 4 Mar., 23, 26 Apr. 1862 (DCLiv NA).

8. Maynard, "Dudley," 96–97.

9. Ibid., 95; deKay, *Rebel Raiders,* 48.

10. Dudley to Seward, 16 May 1862 (DCLiv NA).

11. Bulloch, *Secret Service,* 1:227–30; Dudley to Seward, 18 Jun. 1862 (DCLiv NA).

12. Bulloch, *Secret Service,* 1:230–31.

13. Ibid., 1:233; Charles Grayson Sumersell, *CSS Alabama: Builder, Captain, and Plans* (Birmingham: University of Alabama Press, 1985), 13.

14. Bulloch, *Secret Service,* 1:233–36.

15. Ibid., 1:236–37.

16. Dudley to Adams, 21 Jun. 1862 (DCLiv NA).

17. Maynard, "Dudley," 98; Wilding to Dudley, 19 Jun. 1862 (HL).

18. Wilding to Dudley, 19, 20 Jun., 22 Jul. 1862 (HL).

19. Dudley to Adams, 21 Jun., Adams to Lord Russell, 23 Jun., Dudley to Seward, 27 Jun. 1862 (DCLiv NA); Dudley to Wilding, 6 Jul. 1862 (HL); Maynard, "Dudley," 100.

20. Maynard, "Dudley", 100–103.

21. Dudley to Price Edwards, 9 Jul. 1862 (DCLiv NA).

22. Edwards to Dudley, 10, 16 Jul. 1862 (DCLiv NA).

23. Dudley to Adams, 11 Jul., Adams to Dudley, 12 Jul. 1862 (DCLiv NA).

24. Dudley to Seward, 25 Jul. 1862 (DCLiv NA).

25. Maynard, "Dudley," 106.

26. Ibid., 108–109; Dudley to Seward, 25 Jul. 1862 (DCLiv NA).

27. Maynard, "Dudley," 113.

28. Dudley to Seward, 18, 22, 25, 26 Jul., A. T. Squaree to Board of Customs, 23 Jul., H. R. Collier to Squarey, 23 Jul., J. W. Gardner to Squarey, 24 Jul. 1862 (DCLiv NA); Wilding to Dudley, 22 Jul. 1862 (HL).

29. Maynard, "Dudley," 114–15.

30. Ibid., 110; Squarey to Dudley, 23 Jul. 1862 (HL); Dudley to Seward, 26 Jul. 1862 (DCLiv NA).

31. Dudley to Seward, 25, 30 (quote) Jul. 1862 (DCLiv NA).

32. Ibid., 25 Jul. 1862.

33. DeKay, *Rebel Raiders,* 63–72 (64); Musicant, *Divided Waters,* 344; Maynard, "Dudley," 115–16.

34. Maynard, "Dudley," 116.

35. Bulloch, *Secret Service,* 1:238, 261, 263.

36. John M. Taylor, *Confederate Raider: Raphael Semmes of the Alabama* (Washington, DC: Brassey's, 1994), 103; David Hepburn Milton, *Lincoln's Spymaster: Thomas Haines Dudley and the Liverpool Network* (Mechanicsburg, PA: Stackpole Books, 2003), 37; deKay, *Rebel Raiders,* 65; Mahin, *One War at a Time,* 34–35.

37. Bulloch, *Secret Service,* 1:238; Clarence R. Yonge disposition, 2 Apr. 1863, quoted in Charles C. Beaman, Jr., *The National and Private "Alabama Claims" and their "Final and Amicable Settlement"* (Washington, DC: W. H. Moore, 1871), 145. Details for the following description come from Bulloch, *Secret Service,* 1:238–41.

38. Maynard, "Dudley," 116–17; William Titherington affidavit, dated 24 Jan. 1872 (HL). Titherington, a cotton broker, also swore that Edwards had speculated in cotton for several years.

39. Bulloch, *Secret Service,* 1:242–43.

40. Dudley to Seward, 30 Jul. 1862 (two letters), with attachments (DCLiv NA).

41. Ibid., 8 Aug. 1862.

42. Ibid., 1, 2, 6, 8, 12 Aug. 1862 (DCLiv NA); Wilding to Dudley, 2 Aug., T. A. Craven to Dudley, 8 Aug. 1862 (HL).

43. Bulloch, *Secret Service,* 1:255; Taylor, *Confederate Raider,* 106.

44. Taylor, *Confederate Raider,* 107. Details for the following description come from Bulloch, *Secret Service,* 1:255–56, 283–85, and Taylor, *Confederate Raider,* 106–10.

45. DeKay, *Rebel Raiders,* 188.

46. Taylor, *Confederate Raider,* 195–209.

47. Dudley to Seward, 12, 13, 15, 20 Aug., 2, 3, 17 Sept., 1, 4, 10 Oct. 1862, 27 Aug., 2, 14 Sept., 19 Nov. 1864, J. Latham affidavit, 8 Jan. 1864 (DCLiv NA); C. L. Wilson to Dudley, 14 Aug. 1862, 24, 30 Jan. 1864, H. B. Hammond to Dudley, 16, 22 Aug. 1862, B. Moran to Dudley, 5, 23, 24 Sept., 6, 23 Nov. 1862, G. T. Chapman to Dudley, 20 May 1863, Chapman's affidavit, 29 Jun. 1863, Wilding to Dudley, 5 Jun. 1863, Yonge to Dudley, Sept. 1863, Apr., 2 May 1864, T. Halligan to Dudley, 19 Oct. 1863 (HL).

4—The *Alexandra*

1. Dudley to Seward, 14, 17 Oct. 1862 (DCLiv NA).

2. Mahin, *One War at a Time,* 124–29.

3. Ibid.; D. P. Crook, *Diplomacy during the American Civil War* (New York: John Wiley and Sons, 1975), 84; Brian Jenkins, *Britain and the War for the Union* (Montreal: McGill-Queen's University Press, 1980), 166–67.

4. Mahin, *One War at a Time,* 128; Spencer Walpole, *The Life of Lord John Russell,* 2 vols. (London: Longmans, Green, 1891), 2:360–61.

5. Dudley to Seward, 17 Sept. 1862 (DCLiv NA); Seward to Adams, 16 Aug. 1862 (Diplomatic Correspondence, London, NA).

6. Lord Palmerston to Russell, 2 Oct. 1862, quoted in Walpole, *Lord Russell,* 362–63.

7. John Morley, *The Life of William Ewart Gladstone,* 2 vols. (London: MacMillan, 1903), 2:79; Dudley to Seward, 14 Oct. 1862 (DCLiv NA); Mahin, *One War at a Time,* 129–35.

8. Dudley to Seward, 14, 17 Oct. 1862 (DCLiv NA).

9. Dudley to Seward, 5 Dec. 1862 (discussing letters to Adams and Russell), 20 Mar. 1863, Dudley to Adams, 5 Dec. 1862 (DCLiv NA).

10. Dudley to Seward, 30 Dec. 1862 (DCLiv NA).

11. Ibid., 28 Feb. 1863.

12. Ibid., 11 Mar. 1863.

13. Ibid., 20 Mar. 1863, with enclosure.

14. Lush's opinion, dated 7 Mar. 1863, enclosed in ibid.

15. Dudley to Seward, 20 Mar. 1863, with enclosure.

16. Dudley affirmation, 28 Mar. 1863 (DCLiv NA).

17. Dudley to Seward, 3 Apr. 1863, with copies of affidavits enclosed (DCLiv NA).

18. Maynard, "Dudley," 144–45; Benjamin Moran to Dudley (re. Adams), 31 Mar. 1863 (HL).

19. Maynard, "Dudley," 144–45; all quotes from Dudley to Seward, 3 Apr. 1863 (DCLiv NA).

20. Adams to Dudley (telegram), 6 Apr. 1863 (HL); Dudley to Seward, 8 Apr. 1863, with *Liverpool Journal of Commerce,* 7 Apr. 1863, article included (DCLiv NA); Frederick Seward to Dudley, quoted in Maynard, "Dudley," 147.

21. Charles M. Robinson III, *Shark of the Confederacy: The Story of the CSS* Alabama (Annapolis, MD: Naval Institute, 1995), 173–74.

22. H. C. Allen, *Great Britain and the United States: A History of Anglo-American Relations (1783–1952)* (London: Archon Books, 1969), 486–91; Maynard, "Dudley," 148–51.

23. Dudley to Seward, 14 Jan. 1863 (DCLiv NA).

24. Ibid., 14 Apr. 1863.

25. Ibid.; Maynard, "Dudley," 162.

26. Dudley to Seward, 14, 18 (quote) Apr., also 2 May 1863 (DCLiv NA).

27. Dudley to Adams, 25 Apr., Dudley to Seward, 2, 8 May 1863 (DCLiv NA).

28. Maynard, "Dudley," 147–49.

29. Dudley to Adams, 4 Jun., Dudley to Seward, 10 Jun. 1863 (DCLiv NA); Maynard, "Dudley," 157.

30. Dudley to Seward, 10 Jun. 1863 (DCLiv NA); Maynard, "Dudley," 160–61.

31. Maynard, "Dudley," 163–64.

32. Ibid., 164.

33. Ibid., 164–65.

34. Pollock quoted in Maynard, "Dudley," 165; Dudley to Seward, 24 Jun. 1863 (DCLiv NA).

35. Dudley to Seward, 26 Jun. 1863 (DCLiv NA).

36. Ibid., 6 Nov. 1863, 12 Jan., 19 Feb., 12, 18 Mar., 8 Apr. 1864; Maynard, "Dudley," 165–67.

37. Dudley to Seward, 8 Apr. 1864 (DCLiv NA).

38. Ibid. (quote), also 12, 16, 27 Apr., 6 May, 13, 18 Jun., 6, 9, 16 Jul. 1864.

39. Ibid., 25 Jul. 1864.

40. Maynard, "Dudley," 167.

5—The Unstoppable Ironclads

1. Maynard, "Dudley," 225 (quote); Dudley to Seward, 18 Jul. 1862 (DCLiv NA); Richard I. Lester, *Confederate Finance and Purchasing in Great Britain* (Charlottesville: University of Virginia Press, 1975), 117.

2. Spencer, *Confederate Navy,* 63–66 (66); Lester, *Confederate Finance,* 115–17.

3. Spencer, *Confederate Navy,* 22–27, 66; Lester, *Confederate Finance,* 117–18.

4. Bulloch, *Secret Service,* 1:380–81.

5. Spencer, *Confederate Navy,* 81.

6. Bulloch, *Secret Service,* 1:382–83.

7. Spencer, *Confederate Navy,* 71.

8. Ibid., 70–82 (82); Lester, *Confederate Finance,* 118–19.

9. Bulloch, *Secret Service,* 1:445–46.

10. Ibid., 1:382–86, 445–46; Spencer, *Confederate Navy,* 82–83.

11. Maynard, "Dudley," 225 (quote); Dudley to Seward, 18, 25 Jul., 15, 30 (quote) Aug., 6, 7 Sept. 1862 (DCLiv NA).

12. Dudley to Seward, 8 Sept. 1862 (DCLiv NA).

13. Ibid., 30 Dec. 1862.

14. Ibid., 4 Oct. 1862.

15. Ibid., 30 Dec. 1862.

16. Ibid., 25 Mar. 1863.

17. Bulloch to Stephen Mallory, 24 Sept. 1862, quoted in Bulloch, *Secret Service,* 1:391.

18. Bulloch to Mallory, 11 Aug, 10, 24 Sept., 7 Nov. 1862, ibid., 389–91.

19. Bulloch to Mallory, 11 Aug. 1862, ibid., 389.

20. Bulloch to Mallory, 7 Nov. 1862, in ibid., 387–93.

21. Bulloch to Mallory, 23 Jan., 3 Feb. 1863 in ibid., 394–95.

22. Sarah Forbes Hughes, ed., *Letters and Recollections of John Murray Forbes,* 2 vols. (Boston: Houghton Mifflin, 1900), 1:5–6; Douglas H. Maynard, "The Forbes-Aspinwall Mission," *Mississippi Valley Historical Review* 45 (1958), 67–70.

23. Hughes, *Forbes,* 1:7–8; Maynard, "Forbes-Aspinwall Mission," 70–71.

24. Maynard, "Forbes-Aspinwall Mission," 72–74; John Murray Forbes to Dudley, 30 Mar. 1863 (HL).

25. Hughes, *Forbes,* 1:25–26; Maynard, "Forbes-Aspinwall Mission," 75–89; Maynard, "Dudley," 228–30.

26. Dudley to Seward, 3 Apr., Clarence Yonge affidavit, 6 Apr. 1863 (DCLiv NA).

27. Maynard, "Dudley," 232–33; Dudley to Seward, 2 May 1863 (DCLiv NA).

28. Dudley to Seward, 2 May 1863 (DCLiv NA).

29. William Evarts to Dudley, 15 Jul. 1863 (HL); Dudley to Seward, 3 Jul. 1863 (DCLiv NA); Maynard, "Dudley," 233–34.

30. Dudley to Seward, 3 Jul. 1863 (DCLiv NA).

31. Ibid., 4 Jul. 1863.

32. Details for the following account of negotiations with France

are taken from Bulloch, *Secret Service,* 1:395–406 (Mallory cited p. 397), and Merli, *Confederate Navy,* 189–91 (de Lhuys cited p. 190).

33. Maynard, "Dudley," 245–46.

34. Dudley affirmation, 7 Jul., Clarence Randolph Yonge affidavit, 6 Apr., George Temple Chapman affidavit, 29 Jun., William Hayden Russell and Joseph Ellis affidavit, 7 Jul. 1863 (DCLiv NA).

34. Wallace and Gillespie, *Benjamin Moran,* 2:1182; Maynard, "Dudley," 239.

35. Dudley to Seward, 3 Jul. 1863 (DCLiv NA).

36. John Brady affidavit, 11 Jul., Austin Joseph Hand affidavit, 15 Jul., Dudley to Edwards, 15 Jul., Dudley to Seward, 16 Jul. 1863 (DCLiv NA); Maynard, "Dudley," 240–41; Evarts to Dudley, 15 Jul. 1863 (HL).

37. Dudley to Adams, 24 Jul. 1863 (DCLiv NA).

38. For Dudley to Seward and Adams, see Wallace and Gillespie, *Benjamin Moran,* 2:1201–202. Dudley to Dayton, 31 Jul., 27 Aug., Dayton to Dudley, 25 Aug., Dudley to Seward, 1, 29 Aug. 1863 (DCLiv NA); Dayton to Dudley, 4 (quote), 17 Aug. 1863 (HL); Maynard, "Dudley," 250–51.

39. Dudley to Seward, 29 Aug. 1863 (DCLiv NA); Charles L. Wilson to Dudley, 9, 17, 31 Aug., William S. Thayer to Dudley, 31 Aug. 1863 (HL); Wallace and Gillespie, *Benjamin Moran,* 2:1200–202; Maynard, "Dudley," 251.

40. Dudley to Seward, 29 Aug., 1 Sept., Dudley's application, 1 Sept., Dudley's statement, 1 Sept., Ellis's affidavit, 1 Sept., Prentis's affidavit, 29 Aug. 1863 (DCLiv NA); Wilbur Devereux Jones, *The Confederate Rams at Birkenhead: A Chapter in Anglo-American Relations* (Tuscaloosa, AL: Confederate Publishing, 1961), 64.

41. Wallace and Gillespie, *Benjamin Moran,* 2:1202 (quote); Maynard, "Dudley," 266.

42. Wallace and Gillespie, *Benjamin Moran,* 2:1207; Maynard, "Dudley," 266 (quote); Merli, *Confederate Navy,* 200–201; Dudley to Seward, 4 Sept., Thomas Sweeney affidavit, n.d., Duncan, Squarey & Blackman to Price Edwards, 2 Sept., Dudley to Edwards, 3 Sept. 1863 (DCLiv NA).

43. Thomas Dudley, "Three Critical Periods in our Diplomatic Relations with England during the Late War," *Pennsylvania Magazine of History and Biography* (Apr. 1898): 20.

44. Quoted in Maynard, "Dudley," 261.

45. Quoted in ibid., 262.

46. Quoted in ibid., 264.

47. Merli, *Confederate Navy,* 203; Maynard, "Dudley," 258–64.

48. Merli, *Confederate Navy,* 206; Wallace and Gillespie, *Benjamin Moran,* 2:1208.

49. Dudley to Andrew Tucker Squarey, 5 Sept., Squarey to Dudley, 5 Sept. 1863 (HL).

50. Maynard, "Dudley," 267.

51. Charles Wilson to Dudley, 8, 9 Sept., Dudley to Edwards, 14 Sept. 1863 (HL); Maynard, "Dudley," 267–68.

52. Charles D. Cleveland to Dudley, 12 Sept. 1863 (HL); Dudley to Seward, 16 Sept. 1863 (DCLiv NA); Maynard, "Dudley," 269–70.

53. Wallace and Gillespie, *Benjamin Moran,* 2:1210.

54. Dudley to Seward, 19 Sept. 1863 (DCLiv NA); Wallace and Gillespie, *Benjamin Moran,* 2:1210; Maynard, "Dudley," 268–69.

55. Jones, *Confederate Rams,* 89–90.

56. Ibid., 91.

57. Bulloch, *Secret Service,* 1:435; Jones, *Confederate Rams,* 92, 93 (quotes).

58. Bulloch, *Secret Service,* 2:437; Jones, *Confederate Rams,* 91–96.

59. Dudley to Seward, 10 Oct. 1863 (DCLiv NA).

60. Dudley to Seward, 20 Nov., 18 Dec. 1863, 23 Mar. 1864 (DCLiv NA); Squarey to Dudley, 9 Dec., Dudley to Wilding, 15 Dec. 1863 (HL); Maynard, "Dudley," 272–73.

61. Bulloch, *Secret Service,* 1:428–30; Merli, *Confederate Navy,* 154.

62. Bulloch, *Secret Service,* 1:430; Maynard, "Dudley," 275.

63. Merli, *Confederate Navy,* 211–14.

64. Bulloch, *Secret Service,* 1:445–46.

6—Other Cruisers and Ironclads

1. Dudley to Seward, 2 May 1863 (DCLiv NA); Maynard, "Dudley," 314.

2. Douglas H. Maynard, "The Confederacy's Super-*Alabama,*" *Civil War History* 5 (March 1959): 80.

3. Ibid., 80–81.

4. Merli, *Confederate Navy,* 120; Maynard, "Super-*Alabama,*" 81–82.

5. Maynard, "Dudley," 309–13.

6. Dudley to Seward, 24 Aug., 25 Sept. 1863 (DCLiv NA).

7. Ibid., 25 Sept. 1863; John Comb to Neil Black, 7, 12 Sept., 1 Oct. 1863 (HL); Maynard, "Super-*Alabama,*" 84–85.

8. Warren L. Underwood to Dudley, 6 Oct. 1863 (HL); Dudley to Seward, 13 Oct. 1863 (DCLiv NA); Maynard, "Super-*Alabama,*" 85–86.

9. John Latham to Matthew Maguire, 17, 21, 24, 27 Oct., Underwood to Dudley, 24 Oct., Dudley to Wilding, 27 Oct. 1863 (HL); Maynard, "Super-*Alabama,*" 86–87.

10. Dudley to Seward, 12 Nov. 1863 (DCLiv NA); William Cook affidavit, William Dayer affidavit, Dudley affirmation, Underwood affidavit, Latham affidavit, Archibald McLellan affidavit, Underwood to Frederick W. Trevor, all 10 Nov. 1863 (HL); Maynard, "Super-*Alabama,*" 87–88; Maynard, "Dudley," 321–24.

11. Maynard, "Super-*Alabama,*" 88; Maynard, "Dudley," 324.

12. Comb to Black, 21 Nov., Latham to Maguire, 23 Nov., Underwood to Dudley, 23 Nov. 1863 (HL); Dudley to Seward, 24 Nov., 18 Dec. 1863 (DCLiv NA); Maynard, "Super-*Alabama*," 88–91.

13. Maynard, "Super-*Alabama*," 91–93.

14. Dudley to Seward, 18 Dec. 1863, 16, 19 Jan., 10, 17 Feb., 12 Mar., 12 Apr. 1864 (DCLiv NA); Maynard, "Super-*Alabama*," 93–95; Maynard, "Dudley," 330–39.

15. Dudley to Seward, 25 Nov. 1862 (DCLiv NA); Bulloch, *Secret Service*, 2:260–61; Chester G. Hearn, *Gray Raiders of the Sea* (Baton Rouge: Louisiana State University Press, 1992), 237–40; Maynard, "Dudley," 176–78.

16. Quoted in Hearn, *Gray Raiders*, 240.

17. Ibid., 239–40; Dudley to Seward, 9 Jan. 1863 (DCLiv NA).

18. Hearn, *Gray Raiders*, 241.

19. Ibid., 240–42; Bulloch, *Secret Service*, 2:261–62.

20. Dudley to Seward, 3, 11, 14 Apr. 1863 (DCLiv NA); Black to Dudley, 2 Apr., J. Baxter Langley to Dudley, 5 Apr. 1863 (HL); Maynard, "Dudley," 182–83.

21. Hearn, *Gray Raiders*, 242–43; Bulloch, *Secret Service*, 2:262–64; R. Thomas Campbell, *Southern Thunder: Exploits of the Confederate States Navy* (Shippensburg, PA: Burd Street Press, 1996), 105–107; Maynard, "Dudley," 192–97; Dudley to Seward, 4 May 1864 (DCLiv NA).

22. Dudley to Seward, 1 Jul., 7 Aug., 3, 6, 18 Nov., 4 Dec. 1863, 5, 11, 16, 19, 27, 29 Jan., 16 Apr., 4, 6, 14, 18, 21 May, 3, 11, 17 Jun., 1, 16 Jul. 1864, Squarey to Dudley, 17 Jul., Francis Glassbrook affidavit, 17 Nov., John Stanley affidavit, 26 Nov., Benjamin Conolly affidavit, 24 Nov. 1863 (DCLiv NA); Maynard, "Dudley," 185–91.

23. Hearn, *Gray Raiders*, 244.

24. Information in this paragraph and the following description of this episode are taken from Hearn, *Gray Raiders*, 242–48, and Merli, *Confederate Navy*, 218–25.

25. Bulloch, *Secret Service*, 2:262–65; Campbell, *Southern Thunder*, 105–107; Maynard, "Dudley," 192–97; Dudley to Seward, 4 May 1864 (DCLiv NA).

26. Lynn M. Case and Warren F. Spencer, *The United States and France: Civil War Diplomacy* (Philadelphia: University of Pennsylvania Press, 1970), 431.

27. Ibid., 427–30; Bulloch, *Secret Service*, 2:25–36; Dayton to Dudley, 29 Aug., Moran to Dudley, 10 Dec., Dudley to Wilding, 18 Dec. 1863 (HL).

28. Case and Spencer, *United States and France*, 433.

29. Ibid., 437; Bulloch, *Secret Service*, 2:36–39.

30. Case and Spencer, *United States and France*, 437–41.

31. Ibid., 440.

32. Ibid., 437–41.

33. Bulloch, *Secret Service,* 2:40.

34. Case and Spencer, *United States and France,* 452–53; Moran to Dudley, 10 Dec., Dudley to Wilding, 18 Dec. 1863 (HL).

35. Bulloch, *Secret Service,* 2:42–43.

36. Case and Spencer, *United States and France,* 464–65.

37. Bulloch, *Secret Service,* 2:43–45, 72–74, 79; Case and Spencer, *United States and France,* 467–68.

38. Bulloch, *Secret Service,* 2:75–96; Case and Spencer, *United States and France,* 469–71 (470–71).

39. Bulloch, *Secret Service,* 2:81.

40. Wilding to Seward, 28 Jan., Dudley to Seward, 28 Jan., 1, 11 (quote) Feb. 1865 (DCLiv NA); John de la Montaigne to Dudley, 28 Jan., Moran to Dudley, 28, 30 Jan., 2, 5 Feb. 1865 (HL).

41. Case and Spencer, *United States and France,* 472–73.

42. Ibid., 473–75; Bulloch, *Secret Service,* 2:96–99.

43. Bulloch, *Secret Service,* 2:99.

44. Dudley to Seward, 4, 31 Mar., Wilding to Seward, 18 Feb., 15 Mar. 1865 (DCLiv NA); Horatio Justus Perry to Dudley, 17 Feb., 9 Mar., Moran to Dudley, 9 Mar., John Bigelow to Dudley, 22 Mar. 1865 (HL); Case and Spencer, *United States and France,* 475–79.

45. Bulloch, *Secret Service,* 2:125–27.

46. Ibid., 2:127 (quote); Maynard, "Dudley," 352–57; Comb to Black, 28 Oct. 1864 (HL).

47. Bulloch, *Secret Service,* 2:127–30 (128); Maynard, "Dudley," 352–57; James D. Horan, ed., *C.S.S.* Shenandoah: *The Memoirs of Lieutenant Commanding James I. Waddell* (Annapolis, MD: Naval Institute, 1960), 20–21.

48. Bulloch, *Secret Service,* 2:129.

49. Ibid., 2:129–43.

50. Quotation from Dudley to Seward, 18 Oct. 1864 (DCLiv NA); Moran to Dudley, 15 Oct. 1864 (HL); Bulloch, *Secret Service,* 2:142.

51. Horan, *C.S.S.* Shenandoah, 1–34.

52. Murray Morgan, *Confederate Raider in the North Pacific: The Saga of the C.S.S.* Shenandoah, *1864–65* (Pullman: Washington State University Press, 1995), 126–254.

53. Dudley to Seward, 15 Feb. 1865, 18 Oct., 12, 23, 24 Nov., 30, 31 Dec. 1864, 7 Jan., 11 Mar., 7, 11 Apr., 19 May 1865 (DCLiv NA); Moran to Dudley, 12 Nov. 1864 (HL).

7—The Days of Reckoning

1. Wilding to Seward, 26 Apr. (quote), Wilding to Seward, 26 Apr. (quote), Dudley to Seward, 28 Apr. (quote), 3 May, Dudley to William Hunter, 4, 5, 6 May 1865 (DCLiv NA); Wilding to Dudley, 26 Apr. 1865 (HL).

2. Case and Spencer, *United States and France,* 478 (quote); Bulloch, *Secret Service,* 2:99–103.

3. Dudley to Seward, 5, 8, 21 Jul., 18 Aug., 22 Nov., 19 Dec. 1865, 2 Feb., 20, 23 Apr., 4, 8, 27 Jun., 7 Aug., 13, 21 Dec. 1866, 23 Jan., 14, 28 Feb., 5 Mar., 21 Jun. 1867, 1 Jul., 24 Dec. 1868, 19 Feb. 1869, Dudley to Hamilton Fish, 22 Apr., 7, 15, 27 May, 15 Jun., 16 Jul., 25 Oct., 19 Nov. 1869, 7 Mar. 1870, 6 Jan. 1872, Dudley to Charles Hale, 12 Apr. 1872 (DCLiv NA); Bulloch, *Secret Service,* 2:267–69.

4. Dudley to Hunter (acting state secretary), 9 May 1865, Dudley to Seward, 17, 19 May, 29 Jun., 6 Sept. 1865 (DCLiv NA); Morgan, *Confederate Raider,* 254–62, 294–98.

5. Morgan, *Confederate Raider,* 294.

6. Dudley to Seward, 29 Jun., 6 Sept., 25 Oct., 10 Nov. 1865 (DCLiv NA); Morgan, *Confederate Raider,* 294–98.

7. Morgan, *Confederate Raider,* 296.

8. Ibid., 296–310.

9. Adams quoted from ibid., 314, and Dudley to Seward, 11 Nov. 1865 (DCLiv NA); Thomas Freeman to Dudley, 10 Nov. 1865 (HL).

10. Dudley to Seward, 18, 21 Nov. 1865 (DCLiv NA).

11. Ibid., 6, 15 Dec. 1865; Freeman to Dudley, 7, 13 Dec. 1865 (HL).

12. Moran to Dudley, 11 Dec. 1865 (HL); Dudley to Seward, 15 Dec. 1865 (DCLiv NA); Louis M. Goldsborough to Dudley, 17 Dec. 1865, quoted in Dudley to Seward, 19 Dec. 1865 (DCLiv NA).

13. Dudley to Hunter, 22 Jan., Dudley to Seward, 5, 23 Mar., 30 Apr. 1866 (DCLiv NA); Freeman to Dudley, 13 Dec. 1865, 6, 12 Jan., 22 Mar. 1866, documents detailing the sale of ship's stores (HL).

14. Bulloch, *Secret Service,* 2:415–21; Dudley to Seward, 19 May, 14, 21, 28 Jul., 15 Dec. 1865, 5 Jan., 17 Mar. 1866 (DCLiv NA); Adams to Dudley, 10 Jul. 1865 (HL).

15. Dudley to Seward (letter and telegram), 2, 5 Oct., Dudley to Caleb Cushing, 4 Oct., Cushing to Dudley, 31 Oct. 1865, Seward to Dudley, 24 Aug. 1866 (HL).

16. Dudley to Seward, 14, 21, 28 Jul. 1865, 17 Mar. 1866, Dudley to Hunter, 27 Jan. 1866 (DCLiv NA).

17. Dudley to Seward, 13 Apr. 1866 (DCLiv NA).

18. Ibid., 12 Feb., 3, 24 Mar., 6 Apr. 1866; Dudley to Fish, 6 Jan. 1872 (DCLiv NA).

19. Ibid., 28 Feb., 10 Sept., 22 Nov. 1867, 24 Dec. 1868.

20. Ibid., 14 Nov. 1866.

21. Freeman Morse to Dudley, 13 Nov., Montgomery Gibbs to Dudley, 12 Nov. 1866 (DCLiv NA).

22. Dudley to Morse, 15 Nov. 1866 (DCLiv NA).

23. Dudley to Fish, 15 Sept. 1869 (DCLiv NA).

24. Cushing to Dudley, 26 Sept. (quotes), copy of agreement dated 25 Sept. 1867 (HL); Dudley to Seward, 22, 24 May, 10 Sept., 22

Nov., 14, 20 Dec. 1867 (DCLiv NA).

25. Dudley to Seward, 22 Nov. 1867 (DCLiv NA).

26. Ibid., 19 Feb. 1869.

27. E. R. Hoar to Fish, 22 Sept., Fish to Dudley, 24 Sept. 1869 (HL); Dudley to Fish, 15 Jun. 1870, 16 Jun. 1871 (DCLiv NA).

28. Dudley to Fish, 22 Apr., 7, 15, 27 May, 15 Jun., 16 Jul., 25 Oct., 19 Nov. 1869, 7 Mar. 1870, 6 Jan. 1872, Dudley to Charles Hale, 12 Apr. 1872 (DCLiv NA).

29. Dudley to J. C. Bancroft Davis, Asst Sec of State, 14 Jul., and ca. Sept. 1871 (DCLiv NA).

30. Dudley to Davis, ca. Sept. 1871 (DCLiv NA); Mahin, *One War at a Time,* 290–93.

31. Dudley to Davis, Asst Sec of State, 14 Jul. 1871 (DCLiv NA).

32. George Abbot to Dudley, 15 Jul., Moran to Dudley, 21 Aug. 1871 (HL); quote from Dudley to Fish, 25 Nov. 1871 (DCLiv NA).

33. Dudley to Fish, 7 (quote), 10 (three letters), 12 Jul., 2, 12, 15 Aug., 18 Sept. 1871 (DCLiv NA).

34. Dudley to State Department, 21 Sept., Dudley to Davis, 15 Aug. 1871 (DCLiv NA).

35. Bulloch, *Secret Service,* 2:303.

36. Dudley to Fish, 4 Jan., 7 Feb., 16 Mar., 5 Apr. 1872 (DCLiv NA); Evarts to Dudley, 11 Jan., Davis to Dudley, 24 Jan., Dudley to son Edward, 16 Feb. 1872 (HL).

37. Mahin, *One War at a Time,* 288–99.

38. Gladstone quoted in ibid., 299.

39. Dudley to Fish, 7 Oct. 1872 (DCLiv NA); Fish to Dudley, 11 Oct. 1872 (HL).

40. H. L. Bonsall, *Camden (New Jersey) Post,* 15 Apr. 1893, quoted in Potts, *Dudley,* 27.

WORKS CITED

Archive Collections

State Department correspondence from Liverpool and London in the National Archives (cited as NA in the notes) contains the official correspondence from the Liverpool consulate and the London legation to the State Department.

Edward Carey Gardiner Collection, Historical Society of Pennsylvania, Philadelphia (cited as HSP in the notes), contains several boxes of material primarily concerned with Dudley's law practice after he returned from Liverpool.

Thomas Haines Dudley Collection, Camden, New Jersey, Historical Society (cited as CNJHS in the notes) contains limited personal material, including pictures and articles on "The Grange," the home Dudley built after returning from Liverpool.

Thomas Haines Dudley Collection, Huntington Library, San Marino, California (cited as HL in the notes), houses over four thousand items. This is by far the most extensive collection.

Published Material

Adams, Brooks. "The Seizure of the Laird Rams." *Massachusetts Historical Society Proceedings* 45 (1911).

Adams, Charles Francis, Jr. *Charles Francis Adams.* New York: Chelsea House, 1980.

———. "The Crisis of Foreign Intervention in the War of Secession." *Massachusetts Historical Society Proceedings* 47 (1914).

———. "Seward and the Declaration of Paris." *Massachusetts Historical Society Proceedings* 46 (1913).

Adams, E. D. *Great Britain and the American Civil War.* New York: Russell and Russell, 1924. 2 vols.

Adams, Henry. *A Cycle of Adams Letters, 1861–1865.* 2 vols. Boston, Houghton Mifflin, 1920.

Allen, H. C. *Great Britain and the United States: A History of Anglo-American Relations (1783–1952).* London: Archon Books, 1969.

Bauer, K. Jack. *A Maritime History of the United States: The Role of America's Seas and Waterways.* Columbia: University of South Carolina Press, 1988.

Beaman, Charles C., Jr. *The National and Private "Alabama Claims" and Their "Final and Amicable Settlement."* Washington, DC: W. H. Moore, 1871.

Bernath, Stuart L. *Squall across the Atlantic.* Berkeley and Los Angeles, CA: University of California Press, 1970.

Blackett, R.J.M. *Divided Hearts: Britain and the American Civil War.* Baton Rouge: Louisiana State University Press, 2001.

Bourne, Kenneth. *Britain and the Balance of Power in North America, 1815–1908.* London: Longmans, 1967.

Bulloch, James D. *The Secret Service of the Confederate States in Europe.* 2 vols. New York: Thomas Yoseloff, 1959.

Campbell, R. Thomas. *Fire and Thunder: Exploits of the Confederate States Navy.* Shippensburg, PA: Burd Street Press, 1997.

———. *Gray Thunder: Exploits of the Confederate States Navy.* Shippensburg, PA: Burd Street Press, 1996.

———. *Southern Fire: Exploits of the Confederate States Navy.* Shippensburg, PA: Burd Street Press, 1997.

———. *Southern Thunder: Exploits of the Confederate States Navy.* Shippensburg, PA: Burd Street Press, 1996.

Carr, Dawson. *Gray Phantoms of the Cape Fear.* Winston-Salem, NC: John F. Blair, 1998.

Carroll, Daniel B. *Henri Mercier and the American Civil War.* Princeton, NJ: Princeton University Press, 1971.

Case, Lynn M., and Warren F. Spencer. *The United States and France: Civil War Diplomacy.* Philadelphia: University of Pennsylvania Press, 1970.

Crook, D. P. *Diplomacy during the American Civil War.* New York: John Wiley and Sons, 1975.

Cushing, Caleb. *The Treaty of Washington; its negotiation, execution, and the discussions relating thereto.* New York: Harper & Bros, 1873.

Daly, Robert W., ed. *Aboard the USS* Florida, *1863–1865: The Letters of Paymaster William Frederick Keeler, U.S. Navy to his Wife, Anna.* Annapolis, MD: United States Naval Institute, 1968.

Dalzell, George W. *The Flight from the Flag: The Continuing Effect of the Civil War upon the American Carrying Trade.* Chapel Hill: University of North Carolina Press, 1940.

deKay, James Tertius. *The Rebel Raiders: The Astonishing History of the Confederacy's Secret Navy.* New York: Ballantine Books, 2002.

De Leon, Edwin. *Secret History of Confederate Diplomacy Abroad.* Edited by William C. Davis. Lawrence: University of Kansas Press, 2005.

Duberman, Martin B., *Charles Francis Adams, 1807–1886.* Boston: Houghton Mifflin, 1961.

Dudley, Thomas. "Three Critical Periods in our Diplomatic Relations with England during the Late War." *Pennsylvania Magazine of History and Biography* (Apr. 1898).

Durkin, Joseph T. *Confederate Navy Chief: Stephen R. Mallory*. Columbia: University of South Carolina Press, 1987.

Elliott, Robert G., *Ironclad of the Roanoke: Gilbert Elliott's Albemarle*. Shippensburg, PA: White Mane, 1994.

Ellison, Mary L. *Support for Secession: Lancashire and the American Civil War*. Chicago: University of Chicago Press, 1973.

Ferris, Norman B. *The Trent Affair: A Diplomatic Crisis*. Knoxville: University of Tennessee Press, 1977.

Goodwin, Doris Kearns. *Team of Rivals: The Political Genius of Abraham Lincoln*. New York: Simon and Schuster, 2005.

Hearn, Chester G. *Admiral David Dixon Porter*. Annapolis, MD: Naval Institute, 1996.

———. *Gray Raiders of the Sea*. Baton Rouge: Louisiana State University Press, 1992.

Hill, Jim Dan. *Sea Dogs of the Sixties: Farragut and Seven Contemporaries*. New York: A. S. Barnes, 1961.

Hoole, Stanley, ed. *Confederate Foreign Agent: The European Diary of Major Edward C. Anderson*. Tuscaloosa, AL: Confederate Publishing, 1976.

Horan, James D., ed. *C.S.S. Shenandoah: The Memoirs of Lieutenant Commanding James I. Waddell*. Annapolis, MD: Naval Institute, 1960.

Hubbard, Charles M. *The Burden of Confederate Diplomacy*. Knoxville: University of Tennessee Press, 1998.

Hughes, Sarah Forbes, ed. *Letters and Recollections of John Murray Forbes*. 2 vols. Boston: Houghton Mifflin, 1900.

Huse, Caleb. *The Supplies for the Confederate Army: How They Were Obtained in Europe and How Paid For*. Boston: T. R. Marvin and Son, 1904.

Jenkins, Brian. *Britain and the War for the Union*. Montreal: McGill-Queen's University Press, 1980.

Jones, Howard. *Union in Peril: The Crisis over British Intervention in the Civil War*. Chapel Hill: University of North Carolina Press, 1992.

Jones, Virgil Carrington. *The Civil War at Sea*. 3 vols. Wilmington, NC: Broadfoot, 1962.

Jones, Wilbur Devereux. *The Confederate Rams at Birkenhead: A Chapter in Anglo-American Relations*. Tuscaloosa, AL: Confederate Publishing, 1961.

Lester, Richard I. *Confederate Finance and Purchasing in Great Britain*. Charlottesville: University of Virginia Press, 1975.

Luraghi, Raimondo. *A History of the Confederate Navy*. Annapolis, MD: Naval Institute, 1996.

Mahin, Dean B. *One War at a Time: The International Dimensions of the American Civil War*. Washington, DC: Brassey's, 1999.

Marvel, William. *The Alabama & the Kearsarge: The Sailor's Civil War.* Chapel Hill: University of North Carolina Press, 1996.

Maury, Richard L. *A Brief Sketch of the Work of Matthew Fontaine Maury during the War, 1861–1865.* Richmond, VA: Whittet, 1915.

Maynard, Douglas H. "The Confederacy's Super-*Alabama.*" *Civil War History* 5 (March 1959)

———. "The Escape of the *Florida.*" *Pennsylvania Magazine of History and Biography* 77 (1953).

———. "The Forbes-Aspinwall Mission." *Mississippi Valley Historical Review* 45 (1958).

———. "Plotting the Escape of the *Alabama.*" *Journal of Southern History* 20 (1954).

———. "Thomas H. Dudley and Union Efforts to Thwart Confederate Activities in Great Britain." Ph.D. diss., University of California, Los Angeles, June 1951.

———. "Union Efforts to Prevent the Escape of the *Alabama.*" *Mississippi Valley Historical Review* 41 (1951).

Merli, Frank. *Great Britain and the Confederate Navy, 1861–1865.* Bloomington: Indiana University Press, 1970.

Miller, Edward Stokes. *Civil War Sea Battles: Seafights and Shipwrecks in the War between the States.* Conshohocken, PA: Combined Books, 1995.

Milton, David Hepburn. *Lincoln's Spymaster: Thomas Haines Dudley and the Liverpool Network.* Mechanicsburg, PA: Stackpole Books, 2003.

Monaghan, Jay. *Diplomat in Carpet Slippers: Abraham Lincoln Deals with Foreign Affairs.* Indianapolis: Bobbs-Merrill, 1945.

Morgan, Murray. *Confederate Raider in the North Pacific: The Saga of the C.S.S. Shenandoah, 1864–65.* Pullman: Washington State University Press, 1995.

Morley, John. *The Life of William Ewart Gladstone.* 2 vols. London: MacMillan, 1903.

Muir, Ramsey. *A History of Liverpool.* London, 1907.

Musicant, Ivan. *Divided Waters: The Naval History of the Civil War.* New York: HarperCollins, 1995.

Nash, Howard P., Jr. *A Naval History of the Civil War.* New York: A. S. Barnes, 1972.

Niven, John. *Gideon Welles: Lincoln's Secretary on the Navy.* Baton Rouge: Louisiana State University Press, 1973.

Owsley, Frank Lawrence, Jr. *The C.S.S. Florida: Her Building and Operation.* Philadelphia: University of Pennsylvania Press, 1965.

———. *King Cotton Diplomacy.* Chicago: University of Chicago Press, 1959.

Owsley, Harriet C. "H.S. Sanford and Federal Surveillance Abroad." *Mississippi Valley Historical Review* 48 (1961).

Porter, Admiral David D. *The Naval History of the Civil War*. Mineola, NY: Dover, 1998. Original edition, 1886.

Potts, William J. *Biographical Sketch of the Late Hon. Thomas H. Dudley*. Philadelphia: Press of MacCall, 1895.

Roberts, William P. "James Dunwoody Bulloch and the Confederate Navy." *North Carolina Historical Review* (July 1947).

Robinson, Charles M., III. *Shark of the Confederacy: The Story of the CSS Alabama*. Annapolis, MD: Naval Institute, 1995.

Robinson, William Morrison, Jr. *The Confederate Privateers*. Columbia: University of South Carolina Press, 1994.

Saltvig, R. D. "Charles Francis Adams and Special Missions to England, 1861–1865." Masters thesis, university unknown, 1959.

Scharf, J. Thomas. *History of the Confederate States Navy: From Its Organization to the Surrender of the Last Vessel*. New York: Gramercy Books, 1996.

Shingleton, Royce Gordon. *High Seas Confederate: The Life and Times of John Newland Maffitt*. Columbia: University of South Carolina Press, 1994.

———. *John Taylor Wood: Sea Ghost of the Confederacy*. Athens: University of Georgia Press, 1979.

Sinclair, Arthur. *Two Years on the Alabama*. Annapolis, MD: Naval Institute, 1989.

Soley, James Russell. *The Blockade and the Cruisers*. Secaucus, NJ: Blue & Grey Press, 1883.

Spencer, Warren. *The Confederate Navy in Europe*. Tuscaloosa: University of Alabama Press, 1983.

Stern, Philip Van Doren. *The Confederate Navy: A Pictorial History*. New York: De Capo Press, 1992.

Still, William N., Jr. *The Confederate Navy: The Ships, Men and Organization, 1861–65*. Annapolis, MD: Naval Institute, 1997.

———. *Iron Afloat: The Story of the Confederate Armorclads*. Columbia: University of South Carolina Press, 1985.

Sumersell, Charles Grayson. *CSS Alabama: Builder, Captain, and Plans*. Birmingham: University of Alabama Press, 1985.

Taylor, John M. *Confederate Raider: Raphael Semmes of the Alabama*. Washington, DC: Brassey's, 1994.

———. *William Henry Seward: Lincoln's Right Hand*. Washington, DC: Brassey's, 1991.

Thomas, Emory M. *The Confederate Nation, 1861–1864*. New York: Harper and Row, 1979.

"Thomas H. Dudley." *The Biographical Encyclopaedia of New Jersey of the Nineteenth Century*. Philadelphia: Galaxy, 1877.

Thompson, Samuel Bernard. *Confederate Purchasing Operations Abroad*. Gloucester, MA: Peter Smith, 1973.

Todd, Herbert H. "The Building of the Confederate States Navy in Europe." PhD dissertation, Vanderbilt University, 1940.

Tucker, Spencer C. *Raphael Semmes and the* Alabama. Abilene, TX: McWhiney Foundation Press, 1998.

Underwood, Rodman L. *Stephen Russell Mallory: A Biography of the Confederate Navy Secretary and United States Senator.* Jefferson, NC: McFarland, 2005.

Wallace, Sarah A., and Frances E. Gillespie, eds. *The Journal of Benjamin Moran, 1857–1865.* 2 vols. Chicago: University of Chicago Press, 1949.

Walpole, Spencer. *The Life of Lord John Russell.* 2 vols. London: Longmans, Green, 1891.

Wise, Stephen R. *Lifeline of the Confederacy: Blockade Running during the Civil War.* Columbia: University of South Carolina Press, 1988.

INDEX

Lightning Source UK Ltd.
Milton Keynes UK
UKHW041826141021
391805UK00023B/57